Symbolism of Petroglyphs and Pictographs

near Mountainair, New Mexico, the
Gateway to Ancient Cities

SUSAN A. HOLLAND

photography MIKE ROONEY

Rowe Publishing

Credits:
Figure 1 designed by Christine Ewing.
Figures 2–7 created by Susan A. Holland.

ISBN 13: 978-1-939054-70-8
ISBN 10: 1-939054-70-2

1 3 5 7 9 8 6 4 2

Printed in the United States of America

Published by

Rowe Publishing
www.rowepub.com

Dedication

To LaVan Martineau and his family,

the Chiltons, Jack and Dorothy Hewett,

and Mike Rooney.

Acknowledgments

As with any research project many people were involved with and are responsible for the completion of this work. For various reasons it consumed many years and, regrettably, some of the people I am most indebted to are now deceased making it impossible for me to personally thank them.

Without the long friendship I was privileged to experience with LaVan Martineau (now deceased) and his family, I would never have been capable of recognizing and making the connections I have with this material. The Martineau family introduced me to the traditional Indian world showing me that everything in life has meaning and beauty and made me realize we must open our eyes and hearts to our surroundings. Also, we must believe. Over the years I realized this to be true thus providing me with the determination to persist in this project. It is to LaVan and his family I am most deeply indebted for without their friendship the idea for this book would not have evolved.

Mr. and Mrs. R.L. (Leslie and Nora Bell) Chilton (both deceased) shared their home with me many times since I first met them in the late 1960s. The Chiltons and their son, Lynn, came to my assistant more than once when I was in need of help due to emergencies. The family permitted me to sketch the mountain lion effigy found on their ranch and gave permission for the lion to be photographed. Their kindness and generosity is deeply appreciated, as is that of Mr. Jack Hewett and his wife Dorothy (now deceased), whom I also meant in the 1960s. I stayed at the Hewett home numerous times and was always welcome when I appeared on their doorstep. Jack was instrumental in contacting the National Park Service (NPS) personnel on my behalf so I could visit sites located on NPS property and was kind enough to edit the first rough draft of this work making many welcomed comments and suggestions. I will never be able to repay the kindness and generosity of the Chilton and the Hewett families.

I wish to thank Glen Fulfer, the NPS superintendent at Mountainair for his assistance. Also, thanks to James Boll, Chief Ranger at Mountainair in 1989, for providing a copy of *The Abó Painted Rocks Documentation and Analysis* by Sally Cole.

Another person who has been extremely important to the completion of this work is Mr. Mike Rooney, a native of Kansas, who, after spending 35 years in the corporate world, "retired" to pursue a full-time love of photography. He very patiently accompanied me to sites and took images of the symbols and panels as my early photographs were not of publishable quality. Carrying 50 pounds of photo equipment on his back, he kept his sense of humor when my "over there" sometimes took us half an hour to reach, climbing straight up a hill. He reminded me more than once that he was a photographer not a mountain climber! Mr. Rooney spent even more hours processing the images he took for this book. He graciously volunteered to read the text making very appreciated comments and suggestions and assisted in editing. Mike also spent hours transferring my original text into a format I was able to work with on the computer and has been a tremendous help in providing computer assistance to me as my knowledge in that area is greatly lacking.

I appreciate the support and encouragement I have received from my family. My parents, Arthur and Lucille Simecka (both deceased), shared their great love and enjoyment of the outdoors with me and always supported whatever decisions I made in life. My sister, Mary Lundin, has been very encouraging and provided great moral support over the years.

I also am indebted to the prehistoric and historic inhabitants of the Mountainair area. By placing their symbols upon the rocks, they left behind clues to their culture which provide us with precious insights into their thoughts, ideas and ways of life thus exposing us to their "human" side of history. Special thanks to the Native Americans who have befriended me over the years and helped me in my efforts to understand their culture.

Last, it is important to recognize all the researchers who spent years, sometimes complete lifetimes, gathering and recording information pertaining to the all Indians in the Americas. Their books gather dust on library shelves while the years they spent doing fieldwork and collecting data is often overlooked. It is dedicated research of their kind that provides source material for books like mine.

This work was truly a labor of love.

Susan A. Holland

Contents

1   **Preface**

5   **Chaper 1**—The Pueblo Indians
Figure 1: Map of area discussed

11   **Chapter 2**—Petroglyphs and Pictographs
Petroglyph 1: Large panel
Petroglyph 2: Large star shield figure
Pictograph 1: Lion
Pictograph 2: Katchinas
Pictograph 3: Negative handprint
Petroglyph 3: Large panel

17   **Chapter 3**—Location and Rock Incorporation
Pictograph 4: Hunter with bow
Pictograph 5. Man with cross
Petroglyph 4: Prey mole
Petroglyph 5: Two lions in Abo Pass
Petroglyph 6: Face on corner of rock
Petroglyph 7: Face with rock incorporation
Pictograph 6: Palolokon

23   Chapter 4—Masks and Faces
Pictograph 7: Mask with down-turned mouth
Petroglyph 8: Eyes and teeth
Pictograph 8: Face with horns, earrings, and necklace
Petroglyph 9: Section of agricultural panel
Petroglyph 10: Horned warriors with small shields
Pictograph 9: Ceremonial figure with swallow nests
Petroglyph 11: Small panel with katchina and turkey
Pictograph 10: Rainbow worm and bird
Pictograph 11: Masks
Petroglyph 12: Lion with headdress and heartline

39   Chapter 5—Canes or Staffs; Corn
Petroglyph 13: Cane and mask
Petroglyph 14: Cornstalk, cranes, and flute player
Petroglyph 15: Mother Corn
Figure 2: Mother Corn or Bird Woman

47   Chapter 6—Flute Player (Locust)
Petroglyph 16: Flute player and backpack
Figure 3: Locust playing his flute over hills of corn
Petroglyph 17: Flute player with blunderbuss

51   Chapter 7—Gods of the Prey
Image 1: Stone lion effigy
Image 2: Train approaching Abo Pass from the west
Figure 4: Mountain lion effigy
Petroglyph 18: Wolf/coyote
Petroglyph 19: Eagles
Petroglyph 20: Snake with circle and eagle head
Pictograph 12: Eagle with XX's on its back
Image 3: Possible badger or bear

61   Chapter 8—The Snake or Serpent
Petroglyph 21: Three snakes
Pictograph 13: Snake and ceremonial figure
Image 4: Natural rock formation in the shape of a giant snake
Petroglyph 22: Snake cane
Petroglyph 23: Coiled snake and star figure

71   **Chapter 9**—Stars and Solar Panels
      Petroglyph 24: Star figure with headdress
      Petroglyph 25: Solar panel
      Figure 5: Solar panel
      Figure 6: Large star shield figure
      Petroglyph 26: Eight-pointed star

77   **Chapter 10**—Birds
      Petroglyph 27: Hummingbird with plant
      Petroglyph 28: Duck
      Petroglyph 29: Fluteplayer and crane

85   **Chapter 11**—Shields and Weapons
      Pictograph 14: Rectangular shield and mask
      Petroglyph 30: Turtle shield
      Petroglyph 31: Shield figures
      Petroglyph 32: Spiral shield standing on warrior

91   **Chapter 12**—Miscellaneous
      Petroglyph 33: Deer leg with dew claws
      Petroglyph 34: Large animal with heart line
      Petroglyph 35: Hopi maiden with hair whorls
      Petroglyph 36: Coiled snake on agricultural panel

99   **Chapter 13**—Agricultural Panel
      Figure 7: Agricultural panel

107   **Conclusions**

113   **Glossary**

119   **References Cited**

127   **Quick Reference Guide of Petroglyphs of Central
      New Mexico**

Preface

Traveling south on Interstate 25 from the present day city of Albuquerque, New Mexico, you escape traffic congestion and summer heat by exiting east at Bernardo onto Highway 60, crossing the vast expanse of Becker Flats and beginning your ascent which takes you through the red sandstone confines of Abo Pass to the small community of Mountainair which is located at an elevation of 6500'. This area, containing evergreen trees and crisp blue skies, is situated near the Cibola National Forest and is boardered by the Manzano Mountains on the northwest, Chupedaro Mesa to the south and the Salinas Salt Beds to the east. From early prehistoric times native American peoples were attracted to this region which offered natural springs, rock shelters, various food sources, vantage points for defense, and escape from the summer heat of lower elevations. Proof of their existence is found today in the Salinas Pueblo Missions National Monument and surrounding countryside.

The Salinas Pueblo Missions National Monument, which includes the Abo, Quarai and Gran Quivira sites, is located at Mountainair, New Mexico, which has earned the title "gateway to ancient cities." Abo Mission ruins are shown, top right, with the Manzano Mountains in the background. Since the mid 1960s multiple visits and extended stays have allowed me to locate both petroglyph and pictograph symbols left by the Native Americans who once inhabited the general area. I believe the region has been largely overlooked by scholars, especially petroglyph sites, and would like to increase the publics knowledge of the Mountainair area and anthropological history. To do this, I will present observations and conclusions I have reached concerning some of the symbols and their relationship to material recorded by early southwestern anthropologist. This work is meant to be informative, as well as enjoyable, especially to those interested in the life and beliefs of the Native Americans. It is my hope that through reading this book you will experience some of the fascination for the Mountainair area and its history, as I have, and can image the life and trials of these former inhabitants who left a part of their heritage behind for us to enjoy and reflect upon.

The people who resided in the area are called "Pueblo Indians" because they lived in small settlements called pueblos, or towns, by the Spanish when they arrived in the late 1500s. The Pueblo residents left behind more than just artifacts, they left a recorded history of their beliefs and daily lives. Having no written alphabet, these were recorded in the form of petroglyphs and pictographs.

Petroglyphs are symbols which have been recessed into the stone in a fashion, such as pecking, abrading or incising. **Pictographs** have been applied on the rocks surface as a painting in one or more colors. The term "rock art" is widely used today in association with petroglyphs and pictographs, but can be misleading and too general to be a functional description because of the specific meaning the symbols represent. The use of the term is like calling Monet's "Water Lilies" just a painting.

Over the years, as I located and studied sites in the Mountainair area I began to notice that specific symbols appeared to relate to documented information from early researchers and ethnologist who worked and lived among the Pueblo Indians. Where possible I prefer to use original records from people, such as Frederick W. Hodge and Frank H. Cushing instead of more recent material which, many times, has been combined and republished from earlier reports. The dates I present are relative dates from referenced material relating symbols to ceremonies, artifacts or dates of a specific item such as a weapon type.

When studying artifacts recovered from sites, such as pottery and lithics (which can be easily measured, weighed, and analyzed), you see only the material possessions of a culture. Petroglyphs and pictographs record the ideas and beliefs of people and compose an entirely different, less tangible aspect that helps explain why they lived the way they did in the past, and as they do today. To me, this is what makes various cultures most interesting, the human facet of life. It is important to respect all cultures and remember that their material remains convey messages from the past and, if destroyed or damaged, are irreplaceable. If this happens, we not only lose pieces of history, but are cheated of the opportunity to learn. We must remember all mankind is truly connected. A dear friend of mine once wrote "the thread of life has no end."

Production of symbols and panels consumed a great deal of time and effort. A piece of harder stone, such as quartz, was needed to peck or abrade symbols into the native sandstone.

The concoction of paint for the pictographs was no doubt very time consuming and specific materials had to be located, gathered, and processed. Because of the harshness of the land, I'm sure the early residents of the area were very busy on a day to day basis just trying to survive. They would have been involved in gathering, producing, and preserving food (including the daily grinding of corn), construction and repair of clothing, and water needed to be carried from the nearest spring. Living quarters had to be maintained, as adobe is in an almost constant state of disrepair from the elements. People would have been too busy surviving on a daily basis to have just sat around "doodling" on the rocks.

While the panels and symbols of the Mountainair area had specific reasons and meanings to the Native American inhabitants they are very artistic. In fact, more artistic than in most other areas I have visited over the years. Their renderings are much more than just expressive "art." Substantiating this interpretation is the purpose of this book.

CHAPTER 1

The Pueblo Indians

When speaking of the Pueblos of the Southwest there are two geographical areas, the Western Pueblos and the Eastern Pueblos (see map, Figure 1). The Western Pueblos include the Hopi, Zuni, Acoma, and Laguna while the Eastern Pueblos are located in the vicinity of the Rio Grande River Valley and stretch from the northern Tiwa linguistic group at Taos south to the Piro in the Socorro area. This includes the Tompiro division in the Mountainair region. Much of the early treatises discussing symbols in the Mountainair area documents that the Hopi and Zuni cultures were mutually influenced over time.

The culture of the western Pueblos was not as intensely affected by early Spanish contact as the eastern groups, and "there is good reason to believe that many Pueblo people left the Rio Grande region and moved to Acoma, Zuni, and Hopi to escape from Spanish domination and continue to practice their indigenous religion…" (C. Schaafsma 1994:122). When the Pueblo Indians revolted against the Spanish in the 1680s "many Indians fled from the Rio Grande to the Hopi…Some of these built the town of Payupki on the Middle Mesa, but were brought back and settled at Sandia in 1748" (Hodge et al 1945:299). Hopi ceremonial items discovered in a sealed room in Chaco Canyon, in northwestern New Mexico, show a mixing of "religion among the Pueblo Indians for more than 800 years, and

5

perhaps as much as 1000 years" (Dutton 1963:39). An early katchina artifact and painted prayersticks comparable to those seen in the Kuaua kiva paintings in New Mexico were found in a cave near Phoenix, Arizona (Dutton ibid: 40), while obsidian from the Jemez Mountains, north of Albuquerque, and turquoise from southern New Mexico has recently been found at Wichita sites in southeastern Kansas (Hawley 2000:244; 249). This shows the spread of material items from the Pueblo area, both to the northeast and southwest. Along with trade goods, ideas, and beliefs were possibly exchanged or absorbed between groups during friendly contact. Along with commerce, intermarriage would have aided in both material and ceremonial exchange.

The only pictograph or petroglyph site in the immediate Mountainair area that has been given a date is the Painted Rocks Site near Abo. The estimated time period for this site is A.D.1300 to 1672 (Cole 1984:41) although considering the large time span of occupation in the area, and the number of panels present, some may date earlier. Two other New Mexico sites which contain painted kiva murals that have symbols similar to those in the Mountainair region are Pottery Mound and Kuaua. Pottery Mound, the closest, is located within 45 miles of Albuquerque and Kuaua is located farther north in the Coronado State Monument at Bernallio, New Mexico. While Pottery Mound is an Anasazi site, Kuaua displays the Rio Grande pueblo traits with dates of occupation between A.D. 1300 and 1573 to 1593. This dates Kuaua earlier than Pottery Mound (Dutton 1963:23, 33, 189, 204) but within the same time period of Mountainair sites. However, Schaafsma (2000: 73) gives the dates of A.D. 1325 to 1450 for the main time frame of Pottery Mound. Using the above dates all three areas would have been occupied during the same time period. The kiva murals at both Pottery Mound and Kuaua offer a glimpse into the ceremonial life and belief of the Pueblo Indians. To help comprehend the material presented it is important to understand Pueblo religion and belief.

The ceremonial chamber of the Pueblo Indians, called a "kiva," may be varied in shape and either above or entirely below ground. These chambers are entered by a ladder through their only opening, a hole in the roof. They contain a fire pit, usually a bench, a low platform, and may have plastered floors. The floor contains a "Sipapu," a small hole symbolizing the place of origin and of departed spirits. Plastered walls may have applied paintings relating to Pueblo religion and ceremonies. "In most of the Pueblo kivas ceremonies are performed which no white person has ever witnessed; this is notably the case with the Rio Grande villages" (Hodge et al 1945:226). Kivas continued to be used by Pueblo Indians today.

Nevada

Utah

Colorado

Colorado River

Rio Grande

San Juan River

12

Flagstaff

Little Colorado

11

13

8

7   6

10   4   A   9

5   B

Santa Fe

Albuquerque

3

1   Mountainair

2

New Mexico

Phoenix

Salt River

14

Gila River

Rio Grande

Arizona

El Paso

1 Abo
2 Gran Quivera
3 Isleta
4 Laguna
5 Acoma
6 Cochiti
7 Sia
8 Jemez

9 Sandia
10 Zuñi
11 Hopi mesas
12 Spirit Mt.
13 Chaco Canyon
14 Tonto Basin
A Kuaua
B Pottery Mound

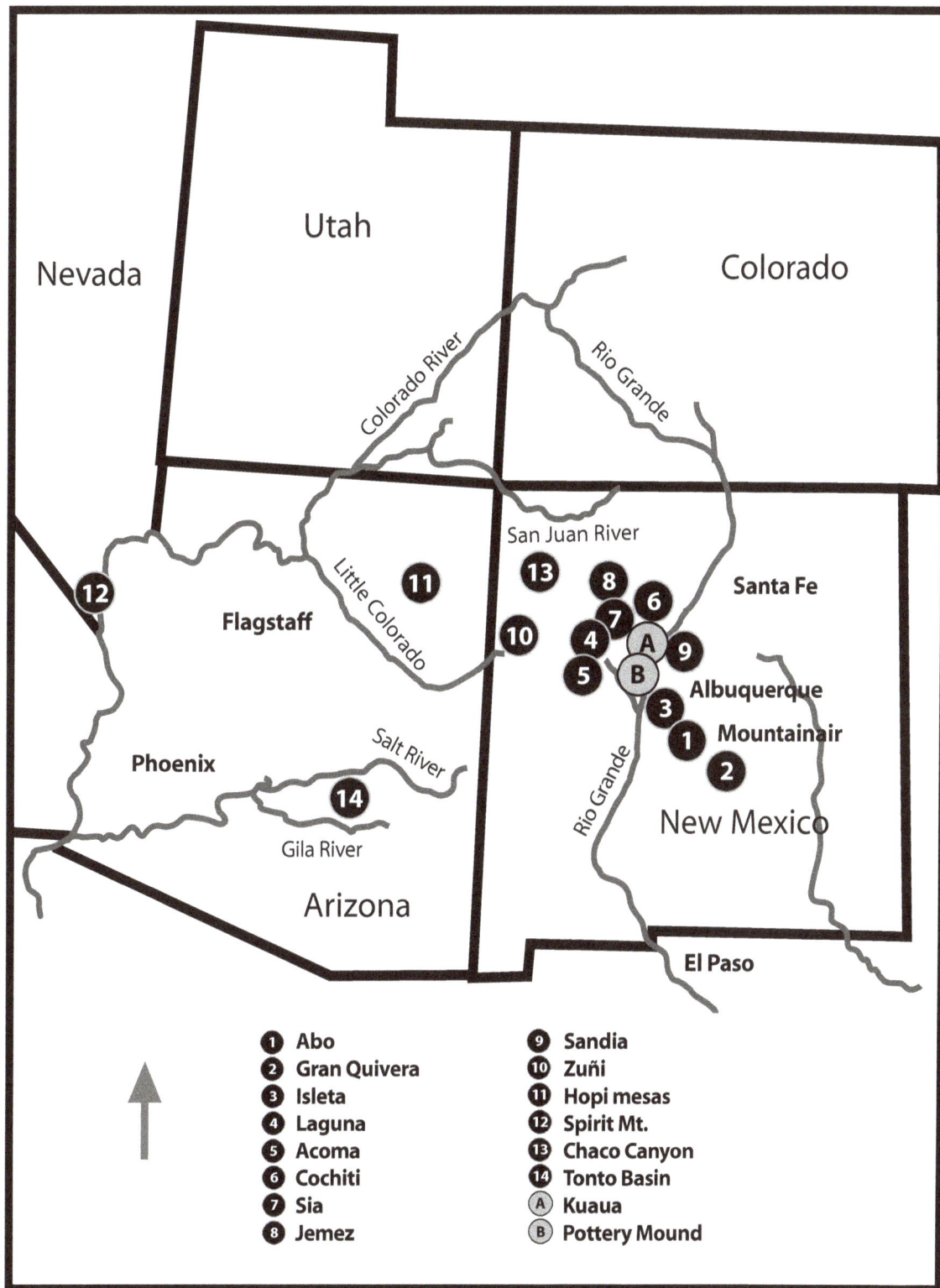

Map of Area Discussed - FIGURE 1

All Pueblo groups have creation or origin stories. Some groups believe they originally came through a number of worlds to get where they are today. The Zuni believe they were first created in a lower dark fourth world with webbed feet and hands, tails, and genitals on their foreheads. After they emerged on the sunlit surface of the earth their bodies were transformed to look as they do today (Ferguson 1985:21).

The Hopi also believe in four worlds and going through changes before emerging into this one. They were transformed from bugs to tailed animals, like lions, and animals with shorter tails became human (Courlander 1982:3).

Ceremonies and rituals dictated life on a daily to yearly basis for the Pueblo people and strict taboos were also observed. "Around the Pueblo is the ceremonial circuit of the directions, each of which is controlled by a god, or a very powerful Spirit. All of these powers must be kept in order " (Tyler 1964:174). To the Pueblos, as well as various other American Indian groups, everything in the universe is connected and all objects have life, meaning, and a purpose for existing. This also includes the inanimate objects in nature like rocks, trees and mountains. The acts of nature we use science to explain, such as floods, droughts, solar events, and the change of seasons, the Indians attributed to their gods and spirit world. Ceremonies, such as the one examined in Chapter 8, were necessary to bring rain for crops, and for "calling back the sun" at the spring and winter solstice so it would continue its journey back across the sky and the seasons would continue. The whole universe and ones surroundings had to be kept in balance by achieving harmony; this was done, and still is, with ceremonies, fetishes, and rituals. If done incorrectly, or not at all, not only would you suffer, but also everyone else in your village or community. Just as important as the accurate rituals was the giving of thanks. Pueblo life was very involved with ceremonies and they had to be conveyed to the gods, or spirits, in the correct manner and at the right time. Chapter 7 will show that messengers, such as snakes, fetishes, and Prey, or Beast Gods could aid in making your wishes known, or help you to achieve a desired personal goal, such as a successful hunt.

The boundaries between the human and non-human world were very fluid and people, under the right conditions, were able to cross from one to the other. An example of this is the Hopi story of Locust and the Snakes in Chapter 6 about the flute player.

I believe many people are unaware that some groups of Native Americans in North, Central and South America share many common beliefs. At times I will point out similarities among different groups from outside the southwest to illustrate this fact. On the other hand a few of the symbols presented are less common and, apparently, pertain only to the Mountainair area, and/or events that took place here. For instance, katchinas are almost non-existent outside of the Pueblo area, so other groups would not have recorded them. Katchinas, also spelled kacina and kachina, are spirits believed to be the ancestors of humans.

The Mountainair area is rich both in petroglyphs and pictographs of katchina images. Archaeologist, in an attempt to date these symbols and trace what is referred to as the "kacina cult," have associated similarities of specific elements to other areas with comparable figures. This, along with probable dates, will be discussed in Chapter 4 on masks, faces, and katchinas.

The Mountainair area shows evidence of periods of occupation from early paleo (Clovis and Folsom) cultures until its abandonment by Pueblo people in the late 1600s (Murphy 1993:2, 60), thus covering a span of approximately 10,000 years. Much information is available from Onate's conquest of the area in 1598-1599 and Spanish statistics which reported Abo, or Abbo (also called San Gregorio), including the two vistas of Tenabo and Tabira (possibly Gran Quivira) to have 800 inhabitants (Bancroft 1889:173). The people of Abo were of the Piro (Tompiro) linguistic family which is a Tanoan language (Hodge 1912:6). Over the years the inhabitants were subjected to many hardships, primarily by the Spanish. They were forced into labor as slaves to gather salt from the Salinas (salt beds) to the east for transportation to Parral, Mexico, for the processing of ore (Murphy 1982:10). Missionaries and the Spanish Crown attempted to Christinize them while utilizing their labor to build the three nearby missions of Abo, Quarai, and Gran Quivira (Salt Missions Trails, visitor information pamphlet). They also experienced droughts and famines in the late 1600s (ibid) and Apache raids which destroyed six pueblos, one of which is listed as Abo (Bancroft 1889:170). The survivors of the Apache raids fled to the El Paso area where the Piros of Senecu del Sur claim to be the descendants of the Abo people (Hodge 1912:6). That Piro group ceased to exist as an organization around the first decade of the twentieth century and today descendants may still be identified within the El Paso-Juarez area (Sturtevant 1979:337).

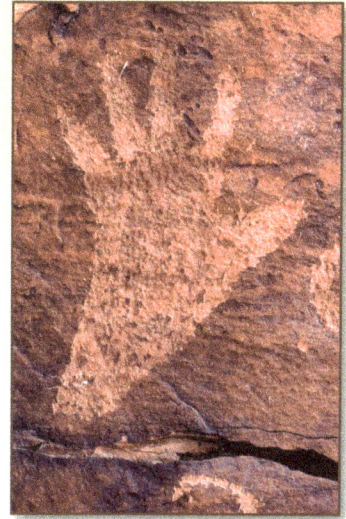

CHAPTER 2

Petroglyphs and Pictographs

The area of Mountainair contains a large number of both petroglyphs and pictographs. Petroglyphs are symbols that intrude into the surface of the rock in some manner, such as pecking, rubbing, or incising. At one petroglyph panel, I discovered a piece of quartz that had been left in a crack in the rocks. The quartz, having one end battered, just fit my hand, and apparently had been used to peck the adjacent sandstone panel.

Petroglyphs are fairly resilient to the elements and are often located at open sites exposed to the weather. Some sandstone is coated with a layer of patina, or desert varnish, a weathering process which darkens the exposed surface of the rock over the years. Removal of the rock's surface when the petroglyphs were placed on it disturbs this darkened area giving the applied symbol contrast as seen on the large panel in Petroglyph 1. Some sandstone contains lichen which may attach itself to the removed area, or, in some cases, may cover both the rock and symbols as seen in the lower left of Petroglyph 2.

Pictographs, on the other hand, have been applied to the rocks surface as painting and are located in protected areas such as overhangs and rock shelters. Colors were made by mixing a binder (a substance necessary for making the paint adhere to the rock) together with a mineral or organic substance to produce the desired

PETROGLYPH 1 - Large panel

color. The Moquis (Hopis) of Arizona utilized pinion pitch and oil extracted from pumpkin seeds as binders (Bourke 1884:120). Ruth Bunzel (1973:859-861) states that among the Zunis, ceremonies sometimes accompanied the procurement and manufacturing of certain pigments. She says kaolin (white) was common and readily available. Three types of black were used: one was mineral, one oxide of manganese; and the others were vegetable: one carbonized corncobs, and a fungus found in corn. Bunzel reports yellow was made from yellow ochre; bright yellow flowers (such as buttercups); and also from corn pollen mixed with boiled yucca juice.

The lion in Pictograph 1 exhibits white, yellow, and red while the katchinas in Pictograph 2 were applied mainly in red which was obtained from hematite (iron oxide). Blue was made from azurite or copper deposits. Two type of pink are mentioned: one being a clay (which is made into a sacred paint); the other was made by boiling wheat with small sunflowers. With the exception of pink, the above listed colors are found on pictographs in the Mountainair region.

Colors may also be associated with objects or certain directions. "Turquoise is associated with maleness and yellow with femaleness;

Large star shield figure - PETROGLYPH 2

black is associated with the dead and the kachina... "blood is red" (Acoma) (Parsons 1966:275).

In his report ZUNI FETICHES Frank Cushing states, "In the North was the Mountain Yellow, in the West the Mountain Blue, in the South the Mountain Red, in the East the Mountain White, above the Mountain All-color, and below the Mountain Black." Cushing continues, "We do not fail to see this clear reference to the natural colors of the regions referred to—to the barren north and its auroral hues, the west and its blue Pacific, the rosy south, the white daylight of the east, the many hues of the clouded sky, and the black darkness of the caves and holes of earth. Indeed, these colors are used in the pictographs and in all symbolism of the Zunis, to indicate the directions or regions respectively referred to as connected with them" (Cushing 1994: 17).

The same directional color association mentioned above seems to apply also in Hopi and Keresan rituals with the appropriate colored ears of Indian corn "set about the altar in their proper chromatic positions" (Tyler 1964:175).

However, not all Indians shared the exact same belief. For example, black face painting among the Zuni may indicate a priest.

PICTOGRAPH 1 - Lion

When Frederick Hodge was excavating Hawikuh, which was occupied from around A.D. 1300 until 1680, the skull of an adult human was found which had had black paint applied to its face. The Zuni workers asked to rebury it saying it was "precious" and was the skull of a priest (Smith et al 1966:11, 254). Also, because the Zunis believe south is associated with red other Pueblo groups may not. It is possible pictographs from the area, such as the above mountain lion, do relate to the Zuni yellow mountain lion, or God of the North (Cushing 1994:25). Please keep in mind this color association may vary among different groups.

Paintings in the area appear in both negative and positive form with the majority being positive. Positive paintings are applied directly to the rock. Negative paintings are most often handprints where the hand had been placed on the rock and the paint sprayed, or spit from the mouth and the hand then removed leaving its outline, Pictograph 3.

Due to their fragile nature, paintings are susceptible to deterioration, even if protected from the elements. Some paintings are very well preserved while others have faded to the point of nearly disappearing, assuming the original was in better condition when completed. Some have lichen growing on them. Another disturbance is the construction of swallow nests over pictographs as they are sometimes painted overhead in shelters, the same desirable areas for swallows. This was observed at the Abo Painted Rocks Site (Chapter 4, Pictograph 9, Ceremonial figure with swallow nests, page 31). Pictographs may contain superimposition, or overpainting of the original. If this was done by the primary person, or by a later one, and for what reason, is open to speculation.

Subject matter can help to indicate the approximate age of some panels. One petroglyph of a person with what appears to be a high crowned, broad brimmed hat riding a horse, or mule, suggests a padre. In the lower right of the large panel of Petroglyph 3 is a person on horseback holding what appears to be a spear over their head. People in the southwest did not acquire horses, or mules, until after European contact, in the late 1500s or early 1600s. This type of symbol could have only been made after that time so is fairly "recent." The same type of mounted symbols and hand prints are in Canyon de Chelly in northern Arizona. The Navajo guide associated these with Kit Carson's campaign into that area in the 1860s (author).

Scientific dating methods for both petroglyph and pictograph panels have been attempted. To my knowledge, none have proven to be 100% successful. Certain petroglyphs may appear older due to heavy patina, or desert varnish, but this is not a reliable indicator of age.

Desert Varnish

Desert varnish, or patina, is common on rock in the Mountainair area. The varnish grows very slowly, at the rate of 1 to 15 microns every 1,000 years (Fleisher, et al 1999). One micron is one millionth of a meter, so the accumulation is an extremely slow process. Scientists are still unsure what causes patina to form although its

Katchinas - PICTOGRAPH 2

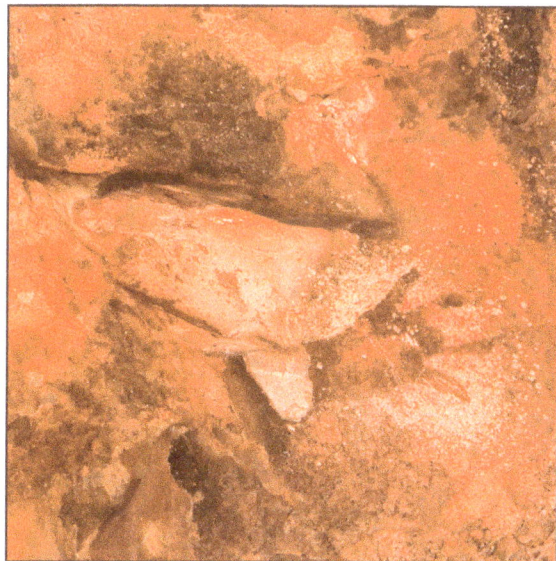

Negative handprint - PICTOGRAPH 3

PETROGLYPH 3 - Large panel

composition comes from our atmosphere in moisture, dust, or aerosols (ibid). This coating consists of manganese along with iron and other oxides.

It is a common assumption that the heavier, or darker, this accumulation, the older. However, recent studies have offered proof this is not correct (Liu, Broecker Feb. 2000; Fleister, Liu, Broecker, Jan. 1999). The studies found "varnish samples of similar apparent age can be quiet different in thickness" (Liu, Brocker 2000: 184). Also, accumulation "rates vary literally over a single rock surface. It may be higher in deep varnish microbasins and lower in shallow microbasins," showing that "varnish thickness cannot be used to provide a reliable estimate for the age of varnished land forms" (ibid: 184, 185).

Rocks in the Mountainair area exhibit varying degrees of patina from black to almost non-existent and can be seen on various panels. Where the varnish is heaviest, the petroglyph symbols show the greatest contrast.

CHAPTER 3

Location and Rock Incorporation

The location of panels and the type of rock surface chosen for them is important although seldom considered or discussed in relation to petroglyphs and pictographs.

I believe the location of sites was well thought out and panels placed in certain areas for specific reasons. Some of the areas were close to villages, trails, and springs with more isolated panels perhaps in areas used for ceremonies, vision quests, and shrines. Among the Hopi and Zuni petroglyphs, some were used to mark boundaries (Parsons 1966: 359), possibly placing them at some distance from a village.

For years the location of panels puzzled me since the Indians bypassed areas that appeared perfectly well suited and placed their work on rocks that are uneven, cracked, recessed, or in other ways inferior to other locations in the area. Some symbols are located so high that a ladder had to have been necessary to reach the spot. After investigating rock surfaces that appeared ideal and finding them unused, I have often "discovered" them in areas I would have considered unsuitable.

Pictographs, or paintings, are usually located in areas which offer some protection from the elements but these too can offer surprises. Some were placed overhead in areas where the back wall of a shelter was available and could have as easily been used. At times

17

the artist would have had to lay on their back working in very close, cramped quarters to apply the pictographs. A couple of face/mask paintings were located in shelters so tiny, there was barely room to enter.

Some small areas have had their openings partial walled up with blocks of sandstone that would have helped shelter or conceal people using them. The katchinas in Pictograph 2 (Chapter 2, page 15) are in one such spot. Since these are ceremonial figures this area was possibly used as an isolated spot to fast for ceremonies or other special purposes. Another example is Pictograph 4, the painting of a hunter holding his bow in his right hand located on a horizontal sandstone surface overhead and above the mountain lion in Pictograph 1 (Chapter 2, page 14). The figure in Pictograph 5 illustrates a painting that has been placed so that the midsection of the figure, the arm and what appears to be a cross, all touch the edge of the rock. This was purposely done because if the painter had desired more space there is unused area around the figure. This symbol is close to Abo Monument and, considering the cross and the white face, may relate to missionary contact although "The use of the cross as a symbol

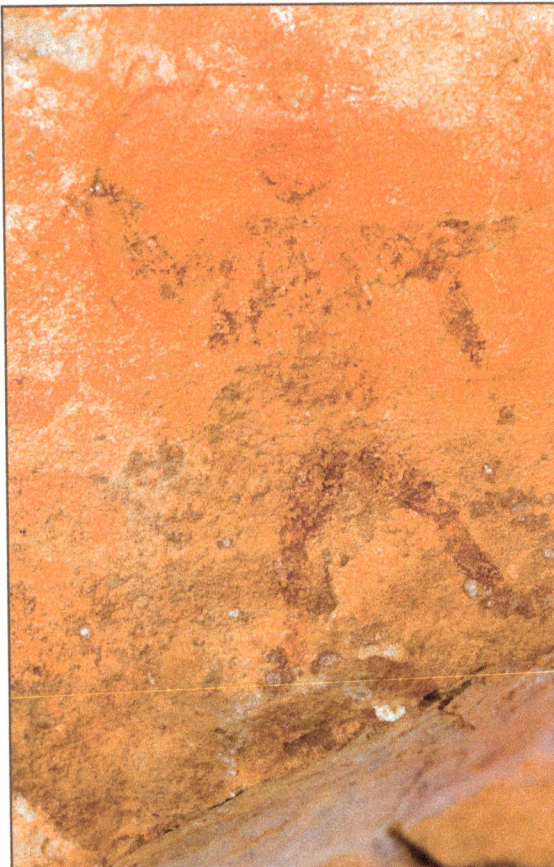

PICTOGRAPH 4 - Hunter with bow

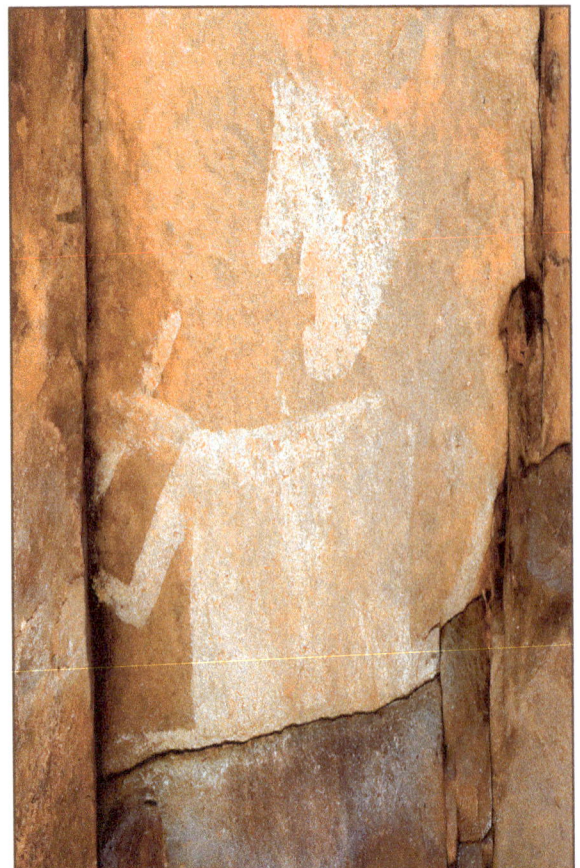

PICTOGRAPH 5 - Man with cross

by the Indians did not mean that it was due to Christian influence"
(Hodge 1945:295).

Often times petroglyphs relate in some manner to the natural contour of the surface, a crack in the rock, the rocks edge, or a recessed area. The pair of feet and two figures in Petroglyph 1 (Chapter 2, page 12; center, far left) were made so they are standing on the natural crack in the rock. The mole in Petroglyph 4 is a perfect example of specific placement of a panel. This isolated, well-hidden panel is purposely recessed into a space so small that pecking it no doubt proved a challenge. Notice the animal's feet and nose touch the edge of the rock. This is one of the Prey Gods of the Six Regions, Prey Mole, and represents the lower world, or nadir (black). He is also referred to as, "the Burrowing Mole for the Under-Land and Darkness" (Cushing 1994:30), having the ability to burrow beneath the earth and lay traps for larger animals. Placement of this symbol in a recessed area suggests it is hidden, or possibly in an underground area, difficult to see, which it true due to its location. Since the mole is associated with the color black, this recessed area can only help to represent hidden, dark, or out of sight. Prey Mole is discussed more in the section on Gods of the Prey in Chapter 7.

Petroglyph 5 shows two mountain lions that are placed in a very high isolated area with an extremely good view of the surrounding area. Effigies of the Gods of Prey, which include the lion, acted as guardians. The area where this panel is found makes a good

Prey mole - PETROGLYPH 4

PETROGLYPH 5 - Two lions in Abo Pass

observation point of the countryside and especially Abo Pass. It is possible these Beast Gods are "guarding" the pass through which one had to travel to reach the Abo pueblo. The curvatures of the back legs of both figures have been given the human appearance, which is especially noticeable on the larger one. The circle above the two figures is a natural circular discoloration in the sandstone outlined by pecking. The present day ruins of Abo are visible by walking a short distance from this isolated panel.

Thus, the animals are up high, looking west, down Abo Pass, and within easy view of Abo Mission ruins. Abo Pass through which present day Highway 60 and the railroad run, was also a major gateway in prehistoric times connecting the Rio Grande Valley with the important salinas (salt beds) some 18 to 20 miles to the east.

Petroglyph 6 is an example of a face placed on the corner of a rock so it appears to be watching in two directions, or perhaps looking around a corner. The face in Petroglyph 7 was made by pecking an outline around the natural holes in the rock and small pebbles imbedded in the natural sandstone appear to resemble eyes and a tongue. On either side of the head, level with the eyes, is another set of natural holes. These perhaps represent the ears.

Pictograph 6 of the plumed water serpent, Palolokon, which is associated with water, or moisture, is located near a large wash.

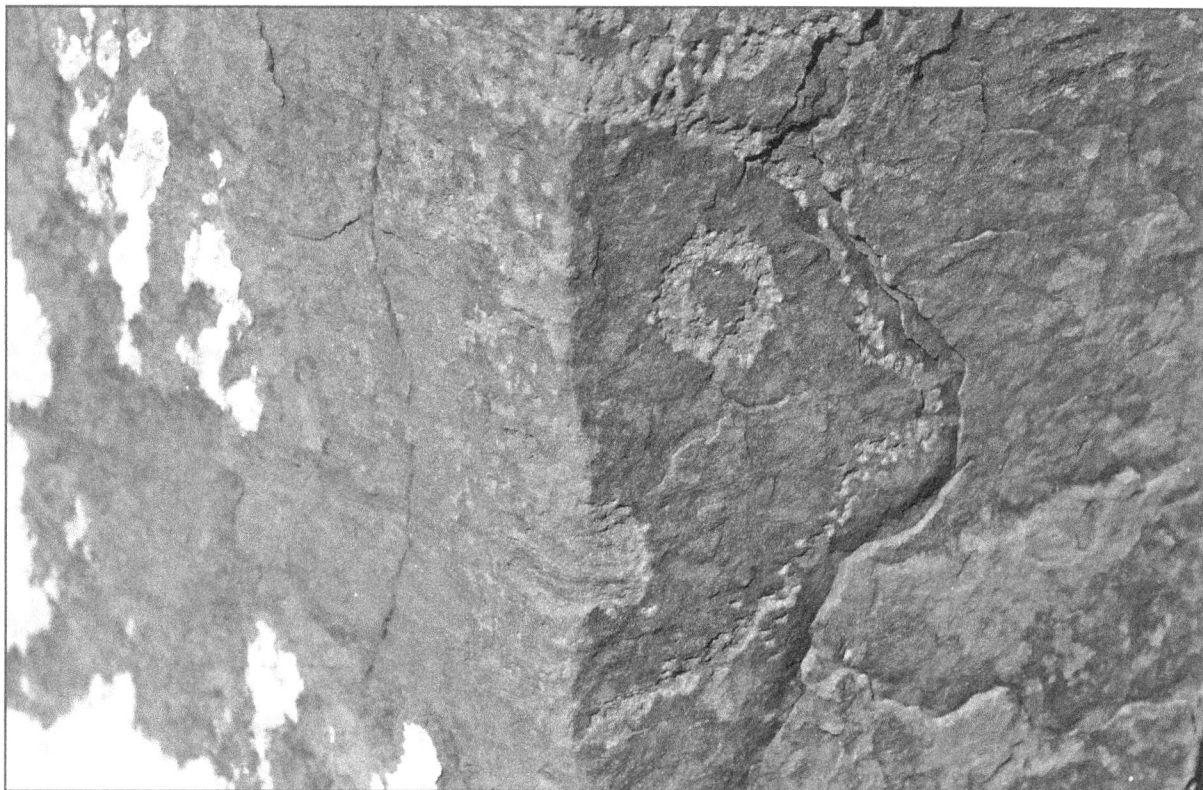

Face on corner of rock - PETROGLYPH 6

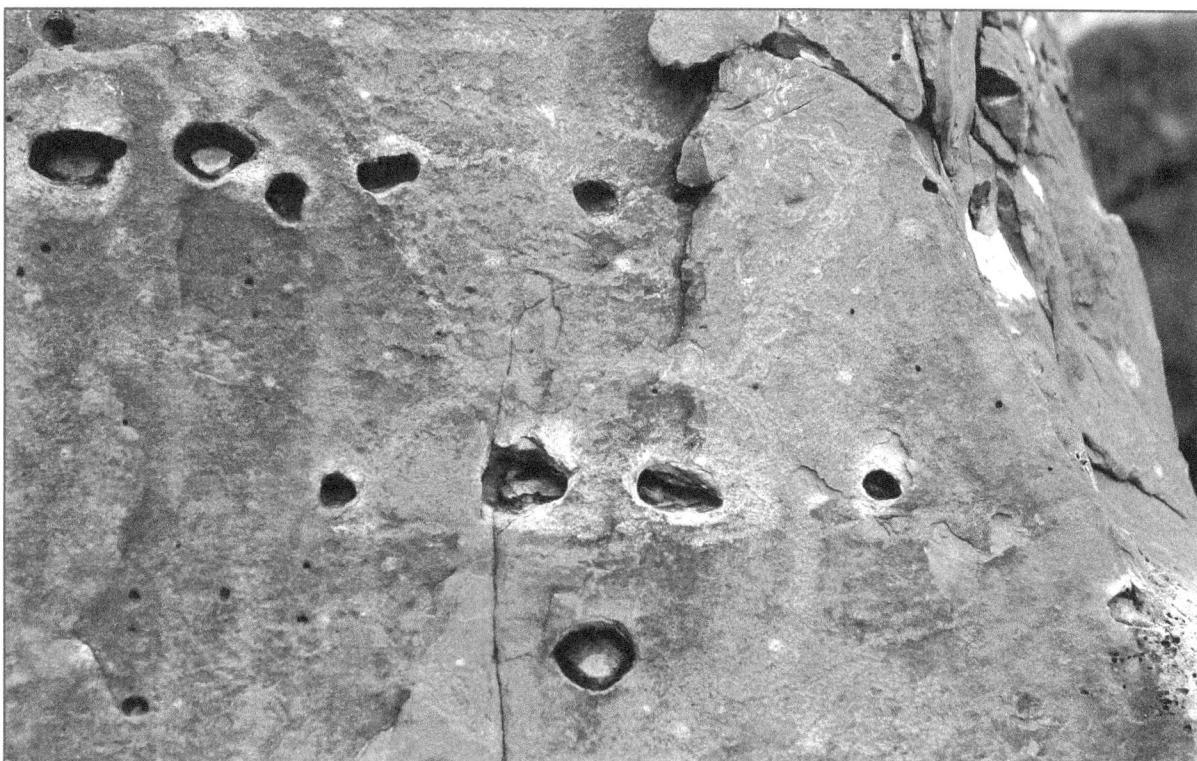

Face with rock incorporation - PETROGLYPH 7

What more appropriate spot for a water symbol than above a dry wash which floods during the rainy season.

The above are examples of rock incorporation, or the use of natural surfaces used by the Indians to help give symbols certain desired meanings. The location of symbols was definitely not random and the desired surface or location used that would communicate the meaning of the symbols or panels and no doubt was time consuming and well thought out (Martineau, personal communication 1996).

PICTOGRAPH 6 - Palolokon

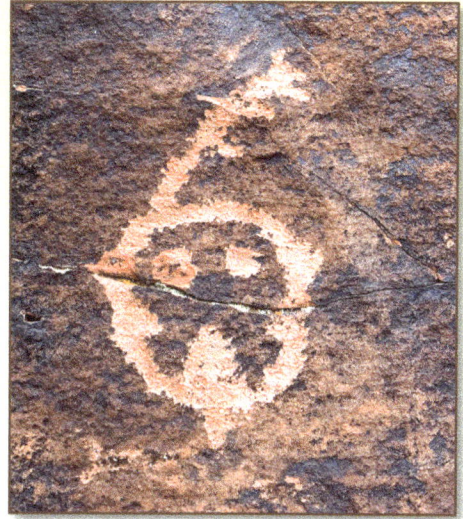

CHAPTER 4

Masks and Faces

The type of symbol in the Mountainair area that has the most variation is the face, and/or mask. These are both petroglyphs and pictographs. Some appear to represent human faces such as Pictograph 5 (Chapter 3, Man with cross, page 18). Others are masks, or possibly katchinas or deities as shown in Pictograph 2 (Chapter 2, Katchinas, page 15); Pictograph 6 (Chapter 3, Palolokon, page 22); and Pictograph 7. Some may represent various clans. Faces appear alone, others are attached to bodies with a few directly to legs and feet. Symbols may appear in profile, others full-face (frontal views), while several are located on the corner of a rock so half of the face is on one side while the other half is on the other side (Chapter 3, Petroglyph 6, page 21). Head shapes are varied and in some cases absent with only eyes and teeth present, Petroglyph 8. As we saw in the previous chapter, natural holes in the rock were sometimes utilized with a head or face outline pecked around them. As pictured in the Petroglyph 1 (Chapter 2, page 12) some heads represent birds, with either hooked or straight beak, while many have facial decoration and are no doubt masks of katchinas. Some faces appear without eyes while others have a double set. Eye shapes include round, triangular, rectangular, diamond-shaped, or concentric circles and talon-shaped. Some eyes are pecked as deep holes, or slits, while others appear to be crying.

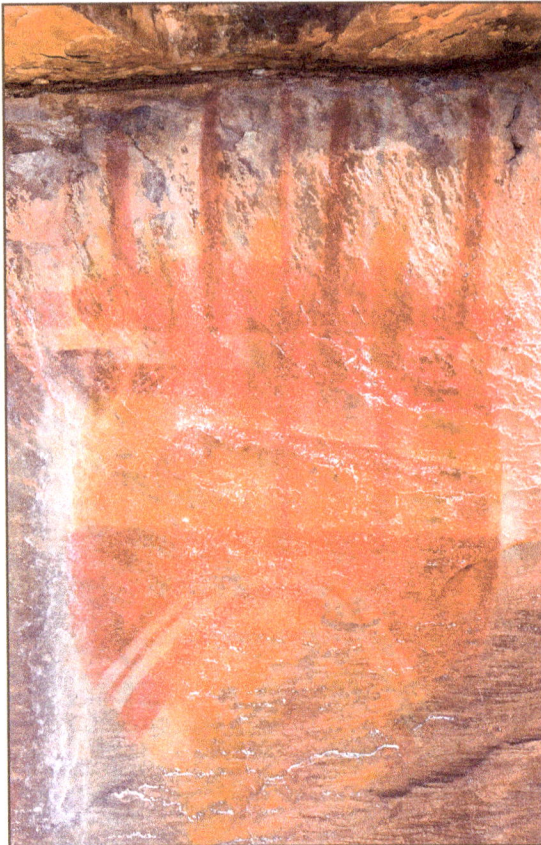

**PICTOGRAPH 7
Mask with down-turned mouth**

Mouth shapes vary with some incorporated into facial decoration. The main shapes are circles, inverted half circles, rectangles, and ovals, while some show exposed teeth. A few heads have what appear to be ears, and others either one or two horns. Pictograph 8 was applied in turquoise paint showing two horns, earrings, and neck strips or necklaces.

Many figures have fairly elaborate headdresses (Chapter 2, Pictograph 2, Katchinas, page 15) while others appear very simple, consisting of only a single feather. Petroglyph 9 shows a mask, or face, with a short beak and a feather shaped like that of a turkey. However, there appears to be the long hair of a person and perhaps indicates the Turkey Clan.

Outside of the Pueblo area petroglyphs and pictographs of masks become fairly rare (LaVan Martineau personal communication 02-07-2000) but in the southwest katchinas and masks have a very rich and sometimes complicated heritage. Ruth Bunzel (1973:905-907) goes into great detail on the subject and lists 106 known Zuni katchinas. New ones may be added while old ones are no longer used and variations appear on the same ones in different areas (Brody 1991:109). Knowledge of some of the retired ones exist "only in the memory of old men, or now and then one may be recalled to mind by an ancient mask hanging in a darkened room" (Fewkes 1903:17). Without any attempt to understand the ceremonies of the Indians their dances were termed "heathen" and hundreds of old masks were destroyed after the arrival of Fray Alonzo de Posadas in 1661 in his attempt to stop the dances (C Schaafsma 1994:135). When the Indians, mainly the Hopi and Zuni, continued to practice their religion, drastic measures were taken to try and stop them. One of the friars ordered turpentine poured over Indians and then had them set on fire (ibid:131).

Decoration on symbols in the area may not be masks or katchina faces but may represent actual people with their faces painted or tattooed. When Juan de Onate visited the present day area of Mountainair in 1598 he called the people "Rayados" due to their striated faces (Hodge 1912: 636) while the Fray Alonso de Benavides' Memorial of 1634 states that because of body decoration Onate called the people "Rayados of Jumanos," Juamanos signifying "a general term for Indians who used a form of body decoration" (Hodge 1945: 265).

Many Indian groups in America decorated, or tattooed, their bodies, including the Navaho, Walapai, Pima, Mohave, Yuma (Hrdllicka 1908:14,15), Wichita, Southern Siouans, Omaha, Osage, Hidatsa, Crow, and Cree (Lowie 1982:55).

A number of groups had katchinas including the Hopi, Zuni, Navajo, and Sioux. Some symbols in the area resemble katchinas but with the large numbers that have existed over the years, similarities are all that can be referred to. Similarities and attributes of symbols resembling some masks and katchinas will be discussed.

Lets take a brief look at the nature of katchinas, ideas on the origin of the ceremonies, and theories placing the symbols in both time and space by classifying elements of their composition.

The Hopi divide their year into two parts, summer and winter, with the New Fire Ceremony in November beginning their yearly

PETROGLYPH 8
Eyes and teeth

PICTOGRAPH 8
Face with horns, earrings, and necklace

PETROGLYPH 9 - Section of agricultural panel

dances. They believed their katchinas were spirits of long dead ancestors who bear those person's traits (Fewkes 1903:16,19).

The Zuni katchina cult was founded upon a group of supernaturals that lived in a village at the bottom of a lake west of Zuni. The katchinas spent their time singing and dancing and on occasion they would transform into ducks and travel to Zuni where they would dance for the people. They used feathers of prayersticks to clothe themselves and lived on the essence of sacrificed food offered to them in the river. They were thought to be the dead who came to dance for the people bringing them food, and in times of drought, rain. The katchinas stopped coming to the people because every time they did someone would return with them (or die), which made them very sad. However, they gave the people permission to make masks and carry on the ceremonies. The masks have great power and are treated with grave respect. When an owner put on the mask he actually became that katchina, possessing those special powers and attributes afforded by that specific mask. One taboo stated that the power of the mask was so great that if a person who was not taking part of the ceremony tried on a mask that he would die (Bunzel 1973: 843-848).

Some groups believed katchinas capable of bringing bad luck. For instance, the Keres associated their katchinas with the destruction of tornadoes, believing them to cause havoc by flying through the air (Curtis 1970 VOL. XVI: 176).

Keep in mind the original katchinas and masks were ceremonial and sacred. Starting in the 1960s and 1970s artists responded to the interest taken by the non-Indian "collector" of such items and began producing them to target the public (Wright 1977:18). Walk into any curio shop today and evidence of this can be seen. Traditional katchinas carved by Native Americans for their own use were, for the most part, from a single piece of cottonwood and had minimal decoration. Only when they became a sales item did the Indians start adding all the elaborate accessories we see today.

Origins of the Katchinas

Where the katchinas and their ceremonies originated is debatable. The Indians of the southwest may have adapted these practices from Mesoamerica and a number of correlating characteristic have been observed between the Aztec, Hopi, and Zuni gods (Young 1994: Table 10.1). During the 1100s and 1200s central Mexico saw the Toltec culture crumbling and its people migrating to other areas, possibly the southwest. The southwestern Mogollon culture shows "traits which certainly had their source in Mexico" (Dutton 1963:197). Adolph Bandelier reported that the Jemez Indians had a book in which the history of the King Montezuma was painted, and also stated that the Pueblo Indians had a katchina to Montezuma (1966:130,261). Bandelier wrote, "the pueblos of the Rio Chaco, etc., were not built by the Pueblos, but by Montezuma…" (1966:155).

Two theories exist for tracing the spread of the katchina and its ceremonialism after it appeared in the southwest. E. Charles Adams believes it developed via the Mimbres influence in the Little Colorado area; while Polly Schaafsma states it was the result of the Jornado Mogollon and developed in the Rio Grande area (P. Schaafsma 1994:64). From the number of masks and ceremonial figures, it was "in existence and active throughout the area during early Spanish contact" (Adams 1991:21) and can be still observed today in many Pueblo villages.

Perhaps tracing the spread of the katchina ceremonies in the Southwest is a moot point and may never be proven. However, the Mountainair area contains elements of what has been termed the Hopi Jornado style (Adams 1991:148) with the most prevalent characteristics perhaps associated with the Jornado Mogollon (P. Schaafsma 1994:74). These styles or characteristics are associated by means of design elements found in the symbols.

Adams (1991: 132) states that the upper Little Colorado Valley elements, from the Hopi and Zuni, originated in the western pueblos earlier, about A.D.1325, and are not present among the Rio Grande Jornado. These are round eyes, no nose, the round head, and a toothed mouth that is rectangular in shape.

The Jornado Mogollon elements include: square, round or bowl-shaped masks; facial decoration including weather related symbols, banding in the form of stripes or dots, feathers, birds or hand prints, asymmetrical eyes, and placement on the corner of rocks. Also included are negative pecked patterns, feathered and horned head-dresses, stocking hat like elements, beaks, teethed mouths, star-faced elements along with birds, animals and animal tracks in relation to the masks (P. Schafssma 1994:74). We will see that the largest majority of the proceeding elements are present in the Mountainair symbols.

Some Mimbres art forms are also present including natural-istically shaped legs and feet, toothed mouths and horned serpent symbols which are found near Casas Grandes, Mexico (ibid: 65, 69). The author has not observed stocking hat headgear in the Mountainair region although horned headdresses, reported to be more rare by Schafssma, are present, Pictograph 8 and Petroglyph 10. The latter shows a pair of figures with horned headgear and one holding a small shield in each hand. This type of small hand-held shield is reported to be extremely rare (Schafssma 2000:33). Most shields in the area are large body shields. The smaller shields were used by the plains Indians (Lowie 1982:71) after the acquisition of horses which required the smaller items that were manageable on horseback.

Petroglyph 10 contains two shaman or warriors located on a flat surface at the edge of a high cliff. Both figures have horns which appear to be exaggerated in size meaning very strong, very power-ful or medicine (Martineau 1973; Chart 5) and the figure on the left has two small shields. The right hand figure has a very elongated neck and between the two is a slightly curved symbol meaning "go around" (ibed; pgs 18,19). It is often the case when a person looks at an object in the distance to raise your head or stretch your neck up to try and get a better look. This figure is telling us to look a long distance as its neck is very long.

Standing at the foot of this panel we face across a deep can-yon the way the heads of the figures are oriented and can see the northwest extension of this mesa which is approximately one half mile away. The mesa has high vertical sides making it impossible to scale.The only way to get from this petroglyph panel to the opposite side is to "go around" in the direction the curved symbol indicates. The remains of a large ruin are located across the canyon on the far

Horned warriors with small shields - PETROGLYPH 10

mesa top. Hence, the figure on the right is telling us there is some-thing **way over there** and to get there we must **go around**.

Symbols may have a combination of meanings and I believe these two figures, especially the one on the left, represent the Twin War Gods or brothers, major dieties of the Pueblo Indians. At Zuni the Twins Brothers play a part in a number of folk tales and myths and on First Mesa at Hopi are kept three sets of War Brother images (Parsons 1966, 183). The miniature shields on this panel are reported to be very rare (Schaafsma 2000; 33) and give special meaning to these figures. Miniature shields are associated with the Pueblo Twin War Gods, or brothers, and were offered to them along with other miniature weapons at hilltop shrines (Parsons 1966:183, 305, 688). The two shields help to clarify that there are two brothers, one shield for each.

This small panel is in a very isolated area with the only two other symbols close by, a mountain lion and a long horn. Chapter 7 will explain that the mountain lion is one of the Prey Gods or warriors, a powerful hunter with important power in the war society (Parsons 1966; 899). The long horn is associated with the year-long ceremonies and the katchinas. This hilltop spot supports ceremonial meaning plus it overlooks the area approaching Abo Pass as shown in Chapter 7, Image 2, page 54. After going through Abo Pass one may travel on east to the Salinas, or salt beds. Salt was a very important commodity and trade item.

The largest collection of Mountainair pictographs appears to represent ceremonial figures and is discussed in "The Abo Painted Rocks Documentation and Analysis" (Cole 1984) prepared for the Salinas National Monument. Painted Rocks is approximately a half mile from Abo Mission and is located within Abo Pass through which various tribes passed to procure salt from the Salinas area to the east. Also, between Painted Rocks and Abo Mission is a natural spring that still runs today. The paintings, located in a rock shelter, have been heavily vandalized but human figures (along with other symbols) with headdresses, sashes, necklaces, bracelets, earrings, and what appears to be body painting may still be seen. It is stated that the pictographs are pre A.D. 1600-1620 and their design elements are associated with the Toltecs of Casas Grandes, Mexico, who were in contact with the Jornado Mogollon; the Anasazi who entered the area after A.D. 1200; and the Great Plains groups, like the Apache (who later raided the area), with whom the Pueblo enjoyed a long history of commerce (Cole 1984:14-16). One figure is wearing a pair of fringed leggings that indicates plains influence. Of the number of symbols painted at this site, Cole reports 182 elements (1984:12) could be attributed to several factors. Cole (ibid: 41) offers the dates of A.D. 1300 to 1672 for the Rio Grande elements of what is referred to as the down turned mouth, or chin stripping, at the Painted Rocks site. Some of what appear to be the newer, or superimposed, figures may have been placed here at the latter date when Abo was abandoned as "the aborigines, when they abandoned a pueblo, painted the Kachinas in these caves nearby" (Bandelier 1966:224).

The accepted time periods for Kuaua, Pottery Mound, and the Abo Painted Rocks site show that all three areas were occupied during the same time period. The beginning date for all three is approximately A.D. 1300 with Pottery Mound abandoned in 1450; Kuaua between 1573 and 1593; and Painted Rock in 1672. Comparable symbols are located at all three, including other pictographs and petroglyphs in the immediate area. Of the three sites, Pottery Mound contains the largest number of paintings that are by far the most detailed and impressive displaying the largest variety of symbols and ceremonial objects. Paintings at Kuaua were more basic and the heads of many of the figures were missing. Since murals at these two sites were buried in kivas they had been protected over the years. The Painted Rocks site, located in a large, rock shelter, has been exposed to the natural elements, vandals, lichen, and swallows building nests over some paintings that accelerated their deterioration. When I asked one of the rangers about the swallow nests, I was told the National Park Service would not disturb the birds so the swallows continue to impact the site. Pictograph 9 is an example of the swallow nests constructed over the painting of a ceremonial figure at the site. Additionally, the Painted Rocks site was impacted by U.S. Highway 60 that was built through its extreme corner with some symbols experiencing indirect damage from road construction causing spalling of the rock surface (Cole 1984:1,9).

Symbols that occur at the three sites listed above are: masks or faces with down turned mouths or chin stripes (also called rainbow mouths); horned serpents; human figures with necklaces, wristbands, kilts or skirts with belts and fringe; feathered headdresses; and corn plants. Pottery Mound and the Mountainair area also share the symbols of four-pointed stars with faces that sometimes have headdresses, legs with feet, and figures behind large body shields. The dates of occupation and similar symbols suggest contact between the three sites and possibly the sharing of ceremonies.

Horned Katchinas

Among the varieties of horned katchinas are: ones with two horns; the long horned katchinas, ones with the horn extending from either side or from the top of the head; and the Blue Horn Katchina.

The Two Horns may be related to the underworld, war, and unsafe things (Tyler 1964:101), while the Two Horn Hopi God of Reproduction, Alosaka, who lived in the underworld, was considered very docile and benevolent (Colton 1959:79). Symbols with two horns are in Pictograph 8, and Petroglyph 10. Headdresses with two horns may

PICTOGRAPH 9
Ceremonial figure with swallow nests

represent ones made with bison horns as the early Spanish observed herds of buffalo (Bison americanus) in the southwest in the 1500s (Hodge, et al 1945:229-230). The Hopi still perform their Buffalo Dance in which they wear the buffalo headdress (author). Pictograph 8 may represent the Tewa Turquoise Ear Pendant Clan, now extinct (Hodge 1912:743), or the Cochiti Turquoise Kiva, which performs a Buffalo Dance wearing a buffalo horn headdress and consider the animal to have "unusual curative powers" (Lange 1959:325-329). Also, the Blue Horns play a part in helping to expel the old year; may act as whippers to rid people of nightmares, headaches (Parsons 1966:576-579), and infractions made during katchina ceremonies; and to drive out evil spirits and sickness if the person could not afford a curing ceremony (ibid: 471-474).

The One-Horn Society of the Hopi participates in the first of the winter ceremonies. "On their heads they wear one horn which curves backward" (Nequatewa 1954:9), and "This ceremony portrays what happened in the Underworld before the Hopi people emerged, and what they did to get out" (ibid: 10). A horn curving from the middle of the head may represent Sho'tokunngea, indicating male lightning and power for war (Tyler 1964:100-101). A figure with one horn curving from the middle of the head may be seen on the small panel

PETROGLYPH 11 - Small panel with katchina and turkey

of Petroglyph 11. Standing to its left is a realistically portrayed large turkey. To the upper left, is a shield figure; the striking or snake symbol is located below the turkeys tail; and to the lower right a bird that appears in flight. We will see most of these symbols can be related to war.

The Zuni Rain Priest of the North and the Odd Numbered Years First Mesa Solstice Katchina also have one horn (Colton 1959: 152,161). The Zuni katchina with a long horn on the right side brings long life to people, acts as an advisor in ceremonial matters, tells the people when the proper times are for planting their crops (Bunzel 1973: 962-963), repeats migration stories, and acts as war chiefs (Parsons 1966:201, 205). A long horn katchina, similar to the Zuni one, is found among the Keres with a "crescent horn rising at the right side of his head" (Curtis 1970 VOL. XVI: 175). The One-Horned God of the Hopi "guards the gate to the Hopi underworld, where the departed spirits go, and the souls on two paths, one for righteous people and one for evil people" (Colton 1959:79).

One figure which may depict a Shalako is present on a panel with three long horn figures, (Chapter 13, Figure 7, Agricultural panel, pages 100, 101). The Shalako ceremony involves the Koyemshi, the most feared of all the Zuni katchinas, along with the Long Horns who come to make the days warm and to sweep away the old year. During the Shalako ceremony the Long Horns and the Koyemshi meet almost every night of the year. The two groups are responsible for chants (some individual ones may last up to six hours), prayers and the planting of prayersticks at certain springs and shrines. Two of the Long Horns described in the Shalako ceremony appear to be located on the panel with it. They have the long horn to represent the long life all people want: a small eye "for the witch people, so that they may not live long," and one long eye "for the people of one heart, so that they may have long life" (Parsons 1966:748).

Facial Elements and Headdresses

Mouths

Faces with crooked mouths and showing exposed teeth are similar to the Heyeya Katchina and his uncle, Heheya-aum,utaqa (Colton 1959:29). One of the Hopi Heheyas, Heheya aumutaka tuviku, who possessed a lustful nature was one of the more ancient and sacred katchinas who, before conflict with non-Hopis over morals, went naked and tried any means he could to catch young girls during the ceremonies. Yielding to outside forces to wear clothes, the purpose of this katchina was compromised and it no longer appears in ceremonies (Wright 1994:102).

Faces with rectangular-shaped mouths and exposed teeth, Petroglyph 8, round eyes and no nose, such as the star face in Petroglyph 23 (Chapter 8, Coiled snake and star figure, page 69), are the types of figures Adams associates with the Hopi and Zuni areas and believes shows the kachina cult originated in the upper Little Colorado Valley about A.D.1325 (Adams 1991:132,133). A fragmentary Salado Pinto Polychrome vessel recovered in the Roosevelt Lake area in the Tonto Basin, some 90 miles north of Phoenix, Arizona, showed this same type of face with a round eye and rectangular mouth with exposed teeth. "Kachinas are very rare on Salado polychrome pottery, which was made in many different areas including the Tonto Basin and the upper Little Colorado area" (Hays 1994:56). Dates for the Salado sites in the Tonto Basin ranged from A.D. 1100 to 1450 (author). This associates the type of symbol in the Mountainair area displaying the same features with the Salado polychrome pottery, made in central Arizona and the upper Little Colorado area. The dates of the Salado time period and that of when Adams believes the katchina cult originated also correspond.

PICTOGRAPH 10 - Rainbow worm and bird

The large down-turned, or rainbow symbol found on the lower portion of masks in the Mountainair area can be seen in Pictograph 7. Due to the size of this inverted crescent, which completely crosses the lower area, it may be either a chin strip or a mouth. The mask symbols are comparable to the rainbow symbol in Pictograph 10.

This down-turned symbol appears on pottery, katchinas and is also used by Shumaikoli (also spelled Somaikoli) of the Zuni. It was one of two Zuni Dragonfly Societies associated both with the power to bring rain (dragonflies are always found near water) and game animals. At Tewa this society cures sore eyes and is represented by the blind katchina (Stephen 1936:819). Examining the area of the mask above the inverted crescent in Pictograph 7 we see two upright lines with a third line slanting down from left to right. At either end of this line is a circle which may represent eyes. The two upright lines perhaps depict the two wings of a dragonfly (it is one insect with double wings) and the slanting horizontal line eyes that are not right or off balance (not seeing properly or blind). Thus, I believe this mask to be that of the Dragonfly Society. The Zuni say the societies home was in the Sandia Mountains where the father of the medicine society originated (Dutton 1963:84), Chapter 7. Dragonflies are painted on either cheek of a face in a Mataski Polychrome bowl, and in the bottom of a Hawikuh Polychrome bowl, both excavated from the Hopi site of Hawikuh (Smith et al. 1966: Fig. 52b; Fig. 76i). Residents from the Rio Grande area migrated to Hawikuh where they lived for some time before moving on to Hopi (ibid: 51).

Seven Sumaikoli shields with this same type of broad-down turned symbol, eyes and other facial decoration are attributed to the Tewa, as stated above. Each shield shows this symbol consisting of from 2 to 4 bands and painted yellow, green, red, and brown. Along with one of these shields the person also had a crook and gourd of water and "thus brought their corn, vegetation, and moisture" (Stephen 1936:821,822). The same curved lines on the lower face also appear on Hopi Shalako Mana, or Corn Maid. On these, the actual mouth is drawn as a circle and the other down-turned symbols are located out from the mouth. Other weather, or rain symbols, are represented on the Corn Maid such as terraced clouds, clouds with rain falling from them and ears of corn. Cree women tattooed this exact symbol on their faces extending out and down from the mouth, the same as on the Corn Maids, and the custom is said to have social and ritual implications (Lowie 1982;55). Since agriculture and food gathering is most often the responsibility of the female this would explain a symbol representing a rainbow, and moisture for plants on a woman's face.

Eyes

Eyes, when present, are also varied. Some, resemble commas or eagle talons. Some are circles with, or without, dots in the center and eyes that are triangular and rectangular also appear. The eye on the face in Pictograph 5 (Chapter 3, Man with cross, page 18) appears exaggerated, as does the nose.

The Long Horn described in the Shalako ceremony with the one small eye and one long eye were shaped differently for specific reasons. This explains the different shape of eyes on the face and shows they do have a certain meaning. A good example of this is the above explanation of the eyes and the Zuni Dragonfly Society (Pictograph 7). This should be considered when looking at all facial features; they all have a purpose and were not due the artist's lack of skill. Symbols that were as well executed as the ones in the area were certainly made with the precision intended.

Stepped Elements

A number of stepped elements appear in combination with other symbols on panels. Some of these have steps on both sides forming a pyramid. The large panel of Petroglyph 3 (Chapter 2, page 16) shows a variety of these elements in various positions. To the lower right on the panel an animal (pronghorn) appears to be ascending a set of the steps. The stepped elements are also included on masks shown in Pictograph 11, far right, as part of its facial decoration.

The stepped symbols are said to represent stairs that lead into the next world, or the "stairway to heaven" (U. Bar Verlag; 1989, 217). This design was used in ancient Egypt as well as in the American southwest. It is found in architecture, wall murals, on pottery, and petroglyphs and pictographs (ibid: 216). The symbol is currently utilized on postcards, posters, and jewelry and is said to represent clouds. This would relate to the heavens, as clouds are located in the sky and can bring rain, or perhaps aid in carrying the soul to the heavens acting as a link between this world and the next.

The Shumaikoli symbol, mentioned previously (mouths section), with the rainbow or downturned symbol on the chin, is also pictured on Hopi shields. It is associated with the stepped design and eyes on the shields which have been colored yellow, red, green, and blue. These shields are associated with a gourd of water and a crook that produce moisture, vegetation, and corn (Stephen 1936:821-822). Thus, they are tied to the clouds and heavens.

Masks - PICTOGRAPH 11

Headuresses

Headdresses

A number of headdresses, beside the horned ones already discussed, are present and range from simple (Petroglyph 10) to the more elaborate composed of a number of elements. Some of the examples resemble "crowns" and appear both on the star figures and animals, Petroglyph 5 (Chapter 3, Two lions in Abo Pass, page 20), Petroglyph 12, and Petroglyph 24 (Chapter 9, Star figure with headdress, page 72). The animals in Petroglyphs 5 and 12 are long-tails, or lions, perhaps symbolizing the Lion Clan.

A variety of headdresses, some resembling crowns, were prevalent all across the Americas and also among many tribes in Mexico. The Spanish reported visiting a pueblo, via Abo Pass, which had four kivas and in front of each kiva stood a black stone "on which an Indian with a flaming crown was painted" (Sturtevant 1979:240).

In conclusion we see that katchinas in the southwest had a rich and varied history and were capable of bringing either good or bad luck to the people. The katchinas were present when the Spanish first entered the southwest and, in an effort to stop the Indians from continuing their religious ceremonies, the Spanish destroyed hundreds of masks. Facial decoration on the masks symbolize certain aspects

PETROGLYPH 12 - Lion with headdress and heartline

which pertained to each katchina and strict taboos were associated with the wearing of masks.

The origin of the katchinas may possibly be traced to Mesoamerica. There are two theories concerning the spread of the katchina ceremonies after their arrival in the southwest, both being based on the design elements of the masks. Elements of the Jornado Mogollon, the upper Little Colorado Valley and the Mimbres are all found in the Mountainair region with the Jornado Mogollon being the most prevalent. The area was also in contact with the Anasazi and groups from the Great Plains. Painted Rocks, the largest of the Mountainair pictographs sites where katchinas appear, dates from approximately A.D. 1300 to 1672.

Because the people of this area were among the American Indians who practiced facial and body tattooing, all patterned faces may not be katchinas or masks, but may represent actual residents of the area.

CHAPTER 5

Canes or Staffs; Corn

The cane, or staff, is one of the oldest items associated with mankind and often indicates power or status as in the Bible where Moses carried a staff. After conquering the Pueblo Indians the Spaniards presented each leader with a cane to show he was an official of the Crown of Spain. Later, with the United States in control, the Governor of each Pueblo was presented a silver-headed cane of office in Washington, D.C., by President Lincoln to confirm their land titles (Waters 1950: 369). When the new governor at Tewa was appointed he received two canes of office-one symbolized the American Government and the other the Spanish Government (Curtis 1970 VOL. XVI: 45).

Among the Pueblos the cane can have different variations with the wise old men stooped, or bent with age, represented by crooks while the straight prayersticks represent the younger, straight standing, unbent men (Parsons 1966:163). The Hopi staff is of different lengths and carried for a variety of reasons usually indicating a position of authority. The staff with a crook on the end, a symbol of life, is sacred and usually buried with its owner; the decorated chief's staff is a sign of office and proclaims the persons importance (Branson 1992: 227-229).

The first wise man of the Zuni, Yana-ulyha, who later became the first Sun Priest, carried a staff which he used to divide the people into People of Winter and People of Summer (Cushing 1988:21-22).

In Zuni, if an official was to issue an order without possession of his cane, the order could be ignored because "the cane is vital to office holding, without it, authority would lack" (Parsons 1966:327). At Oraibi and Walpi crooks are found on the altars of the Antelope Priests (Fewkes 1900: 981) and in the Oraibi Singers Society the crook is touched to ask for a long and thriving life (Parsons 1966:328). At Walpi, after a youth's initiation into the Agave Society, he was presented a crook feather-stick to keep for life. This stick was very sacred and buried with him at death (ibid: 325).

The crooked staff is carried by some Pueblo katchinas while others belonged to the Rain Chiefs. The Zuni katchina Old Salt Woman actually borrowed a crook from the Rain Priest to bring the rain (Bunzel: 1973, 1032; plate 42a). During some ceremonies Orge katchinas carry long staffs with crooks to catch the bad children (Branson 1992:16); while the crooks in Hopi mythology would be used to hook children by the neck with threats to carry them off and roast them (Curtis 1970 VOL. XII-a:168).

When the Pautiwa Katchina arrives at the Zuni winter ceremonies he delivers the crooks for the most important ceremonies that will be held in the new year thereby controlling the ceremonial calendar since no ritual can be held unless he delivers a crook for it. "No katchina may come to Zuni unless Pautiwa sends him" (Bunzel 1992: 909). Feathered staffs may summon spirits of members to kivas and the staffs may be posted at sunrise and removed at sunset (Parsons 1996: 327), like our present day flags.

The use of crooks and staffs by various Indian tribes has been recorded through history since prehistoric times. Thousands of years ago a great Cheyenne medicine man held a long staff with which he parted a large body of water as he led his people from their enemies into a new beautiful country (Dorsey 1971:37). The Southern Paiute God, Toovuts, used a staff to part water (Martineau 1992:23). Many crooks were found at Pueblo Bonito, New Mexico, dating between A.D. 920 and 1120, where they were used in germination ceremonies and were a literal "staff of life," curved at one end like any other cane (Tyler 1964:127). When Onate visited the Wichita Indians of the Great Plains around 1600 he was impressed by the way the tribe complied with the wishes of the chief who "carried a staff as a symbol of his authority" (Wedel 1988:21). Stylized human figures with staffs, referred to by Acomas as "directional men," guarded the cardinal directions and were found at Pottery Mound (Hibben 1975:56-57). In Mexican legend, Quetzalcoatl yields a staff striking one of his three brothers, Tezcatlipoca, into the sea (Taube 1993:34). A 1903-1904 photograph recorded Blackfeet Indians, members of the Horn Society, performing important rituals at a Sun Dance in Alberta, Canada, holding both staffs and crooks. Three straight

Cane and mask - PETROGLYPH 13

staffs and a number of crooks, some measuring close to 10 feet long, are pictured (Scriver 1990:246-247).

Crooks were "fed" after placed on altars by being sprinkled with sacred cornmeal (Fewkes 1900:27). The type of wood, pigments, and feathers used on the Pueblos decorated staffs or crooks all had a specific meaning. Cottonwood (Parsons 1966:571) and willow, which grows near the water, are associated with the rain or water societies. Pigments may be associated with various directions or items. Feathers were correlated to the characteristics of that bird. For example, swift hunters like the eagle and hawk had their feathers used by warriors or leaders. Chaparral jays group together and fly in aimless directions so "Zuni War chiefs would bury its stick-mounted feather near the enemy to rob them of their wits" (ibid: 274-275).

The type of crook commonly found on panels in the Mountainair area is shown in Petroglyph 13. It is associated with a face, possibly a katchina mask. Crooks, among other symbols, are also associated with human foot and hand prints, birds, and deer forelegs with the hooves and dew claws showing.

Petroglyph 22 (Chapter 8, Snake cane, page 66) shows a cane that actually has a snake incorporated into it. At the end of the hooked handle is the snake's head, the body of the cane being the snake's body, and the tip of the cane the tail. The zigzag motion of the snake's body represents movement, lightning, or flowing of water; and Hopi Indians carved their canes in the forms of a water serpent (Waters 1950:369). This type of symbol dates back to Roman times when the rapid movement of the planet Mercury was observed and named after the Greek winged god Mercury who carried a staff with entwined serpents (Chartrand III 1982:230), the Cadeus. The same symbol, combining the serpent and staff, the Asclepius, is used today to indicate healing by physicians. Thus the art of healing may be associated with fertility, or fruitfulness whether it is mankind or crops.

One of the fertility symbols at Walpi is a rain, or water rattle, which in turn is attached to a crook. The crook is decorated with curved thorns and an eagle feather. The thorns are said to "hook the clouds this way (to Walpi) from all directions" (Stephen 1936:772). Hooking the clouds would represent holding onto them or bringing them down to earth to bring rain for crops and germination or reproduction of crops. Corn, or maize, was grown in the southwest for thousands of years and was the staple of the Pueblo diet. Stocks of corn, as the one shown in Petroglyph 14 with the ears and tassels visible, are found on many panels in the area. Corn-bearing stalks are "tokens of growth" (Parsons 1996:481) and the Pueblo people thought "that their bodies were basically composed of corn" (Tyler 1964:145).

PETROGLYPH 14
Cornstalk, cranes, and flute player

CORN

Ancient maize, discovered at Bat Cave in west central New Mexico, provided archeologist with proof of the development of the grain (Wormington 1957:174) into our present day corn. In the same area the digging stick, the main agricultural tool, was present as early as 5000 to 2000 B.C. (Dutton 1963:190). Besides being a staple food, corn played an important and varied role in Pueblo life. In purification rites if the Keres, kernels of corn represented the souls, or hearts, of the people and when examined by the shaman, if the grains were perfect and unbroken indicated there would be no sickness or bad luck. Each person was given one grain, which represents his or her new heart or soul, which that person swallowed (Curtis 1970 VOL. XVI;234-5). When curing a person of witchcraft the patient's heart was symbolized by a kernel of corn and, if in good condition, meant the person would recover and live. However, if the corn was damaged or moldy the person would continue to be sick and possibly even die (Parsons 1996: 710-713). The soul of a witch or sorcerer was sometimes indicated by a violet colored ear of corn and the soul of a good person by a blue ear (Bandelier 1975:283-284).

Corn was one of the staples for the Pueblo people and for it to grow the life-giving rains had to fall to earth and ceremonies connected with reproduction and fertility were most important. In Chapter 8 we will see that crop production was the reason for the Sun Worship Ceremonies of the Hopi. The ceremonies combined the idea of the earth receiving rain from the sky and warmth from the sun to make the soil fertile for crops, mainly corn, to grow (Fewkes 1920:501). The earth is Mother Earth, or female, and the rain which falls from the heavens is male. "When they have intercourse, we get rain, for that is the fertilizing fluid. All vegetation is the offspring of the earth…" (Tyler 1964:100). Corn is also considered female and one of the most important objects related to ceremonies is an ear of corn called Mother Corn (Titiev 1992:103). Pueblo groups recorded as recognizing Mother Corn are the Acoma, Laguna, Cochiti, Sia, and Santa Ana (Tyler 1964:117-118). It is reported the only time Corn Mother was observed in a drawing was at Acoma in the form of "a bird woman" (ibid:122).

I believe Corn Mother, or a depiction of her, is represented in the Mountainair Petroglyph 15, Figure 2. On examining the symbols closely we see there are three figures associated with a stalk of maize. The figure on the left closest to the corn stalk is definitely female (Mother Corn) with a very large breast and the round head and long beak of a bird, bird woman. The hand of the figure is touching a line that extends from the figures' beak to the corn. Behind

PETROGLYPH 15 - Mother Corn

the female is a male that has both hands on the female and, by a 3rd line connecting the two, appears to be having intercourse with the female, representing fertilization. The head of the male is elongated with a hooked beak, or snout, possibly representing the mask of a katchina. The third figure, to the right of the corn stalk, also has an elongated head and has its knee bent as if dancing and the body appears very thick or fat indicating abundant food and the hump on the back may indicate a full pack as with the flute player.

To relate the similarities of this panel to Mother Corn we need to examine information concerning the Earth Goddess, or Mother Corn. Hamilton Tyler in his book "Pueblo Gods and Myths" (1964:116-124) provides us with the following information. Corn Mother leaves the underworld coming into the daylight upon earth long enough to give mankind agriculture and planting bits of her heart which became corn. Thus, she represents not only life in the form of food but also life-giving power. She is also associated with the well being of man by producing food to keep him healthy by giving him a full stomach. After introducing agriculture, Mother Corn returned to the underworld to await the return of man after his life ended, so is also associated with death. As rain fertilizes the crops of earth, the male figure appears to be having intercourse with the female and impregnating her making her fertile to reproduce. Ot'set, Corn Mother of the Sia, said "This corn is my heart and it shall be to my people as milk from my breasts" (Stevenson 1894:39). To the Hopi she was the mother of everything living on the earth and "plants suck from her breast a nourishing liquid" (Tyler 1964:133) passing it on to man and animals in the form of plants for food. Thus, she is the mother of ALL LIFE keeping us healthy and our stomachs full with food.

With the above information again examine the symbols in Petroglyph 15 and Figure 2. We see the male figure fertilizing the female figure, corn, to make her (it) reproduce thereby nourishing all life on earth. The large breast indicates milk, or the nourishing liquid, which she passes on to all life. The female's round head resembles that of a bird, Bird Woman, as at Acoma (above paragraph). The object connecting her beak and the corn stalk may represent a straw, or reed, to represent sucking life giving nourishment. The figure at the right appears very fat representing the well-fed fat body of mankind which is the result of Mother Corn and her life giving powers.

To the Keres the feathered corn fetish possessed great power and "is a most important object, representing at once the heart of his life, and at the same time the heart of his mother-goddess, Iyatiku" (Tyler 1964:123). One of the main ceremonial objects to the Cochiti medicine man was his corn fetish that was an intact ear of blue corn, also called a "mother" to which various feathers were attached. Also, unhusked "corn mothers" were placed in storage rooms with corn (Lange 1959:258-259;332).

The Zuni, who use various colored corn for their ceremonies, also believed it was a gift of the gods. To them it represented "Earth Mother, rains, and vegetation, including all that supplies physical nourishment to man, …the life-giving or soul power…" (Tyler 1964:123). Corn is the main item in many of their rituals and was delivered to them from the underworld ever four years by the great-feathered serpent. Ears of corn were carried by dancers and members of one of the oldest Zuni societies used the corn husks to decorate their heads (Stevenson 1915:99-100).

The Zuni relationship with their plants, including corn, is very complex and involved. They consider their plants alive, communicate with them, and believe the plants answer. Their Star People, who were originally human, dropped some of the plants to Mother Earth for it was she who originally gave plants to the stars before they departed earth to reside in the heavens. The Zuni use the blue-green color of vegetation to resemble fruitfulness in their sacred dance-kilts and ceremonial objects (Stevenson 1915:36) .

In Hopi mythology when the people had only small animals to eat, such as mice, cornmeal was shaped into effigies of larger animals and placed in the shrine of Tihkuyi where she turned the figures into larger live

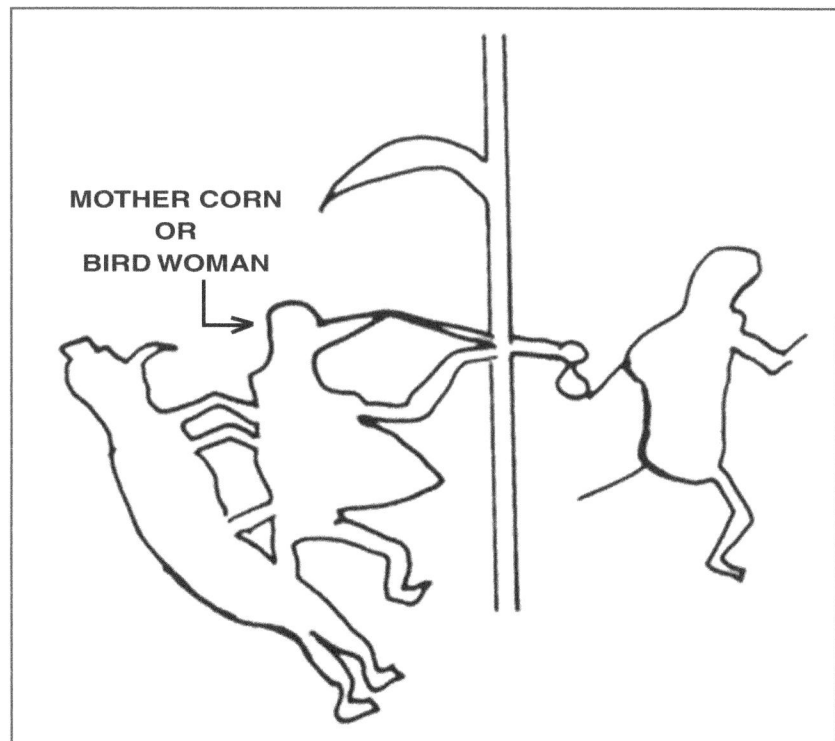

Mother Corn or Bird Woman - FIGURE 2

animals for food for the people (Curtis 1970 VOL. XII-a:191). At sunrise the Hopi make daily offerings of sacred cornmeal to the sun for good luck and a long life; they use it to pacify snakes caught for their Snake Dances; to draw a line across the path into their village to indicate newcomers may not enter; and white corn grains are rubbed into the hair of a deceased person (ibid: 36; 140; 158; 39). The Hopi also make a thin solution that consists of finely ground blue corn meal and water and then bake it on a heated stone. This paper-thin bread, piki, is made into rolls while still warm and is used at occasions such as weddings. When males fast in the kivas to prepare for katchina ceremonies their only food is the piki bread which they crumble in water and eat (Frank Ami personal communication 1993). To open the kivas for the katchinas arrival cornmeal is sprinkled in the four directions, thus making roads over which they may enter (Titiev 1992:110). There seems to be no variance between the use of corn meal and pollen with the latter being blown up into the air to reach the Spirits. Corn meal/pollen appear to represent ones existence and liveliness and not real food (Parsons 1996: 294-296). Thus, they play a major role in almost every aspect of ones life from birth to death and after.

As mentioned in Chapter 1, famines and droughts effected the Pueblo area in the late 1600s. A severe drought began around 1666 and for at least three years there were no crops resulting in the starvation of hundreds of Indians (Vivian 1979:29,30). Other droughts in the southwest were also recorded. The Hopi recorded one in 1862 and after three unproductive years people were reduced to such means as going through midden (trash) areas searching for old bones to boil for food. This forced many Hopi to leave their homes and join other tribes for survival (Curtis 1970 VOL. XII-a; 10-11).

To reiterate; Pueblo life revolved around corn and its importance cannot be overstressed. Not only was it an important staple food but was also involved in almost every, if not every, aspect of life and death. Mother Corn, which brought life to her people, was most important and the sacred fetish of a perfect ear of corn existed among many Pueblo groups. Ceremonies to her to produce rainfall, which resulted in the production and growth of all crops, were crucial to ones existence.

CHAPTER 6

Flute Player (Locust)

"That 'humpbacked flute player' so intriguing to the archaeologist in the southwest is Locust" (Parsons 1966:192).

Whole books have been dedicated to the humpbacked flute player, also called Kokopelli, Petroglyph 16. More than one role may be assigned to this symbol but the insect Locust, in the form of the humpbacked flute player, is very important in the Hopi emergence myth (Sliefer 1994:154). Locust was very brave and the first one to emerge from the sipapu (in the kiva floor) while the Cloud Chiefs shot lightning bolts at him (Titiev 1992:130). Unaffected by the lightning Locust continued to play the flute while seeking the entrance to the upper world (Slifer 1994:134).

In Acoma (Tyler 1964:104) and Sia (or Zia) mythology, Locust was responsible for man reaching this world. The Sia say when Ot'set, mother of all things, carrying her sack of star people, was accompanied by the birds, snakes, animals and when they reached the top of the reed through which they were going to pass into this world from the one below, they found it blocked by solid earth. Ot'set called Locust and asked him to make a door for all to pass through. Locust began working with his feet and when he opened the hole he looked through, said all looked good, and everybody passed through into the upper world (Stevenson 1894:36-37).

PETROGLYPH 16
Flute player and backpack

The flute player may or may not be portrayed with a humpback. The hump represents a back pack in which are carried items pertaining to the type of flute player depicted. The flute may be used to attract butterflies and flowers symbolizing the beauty in nature to the Zuni (Stevenson 1915: 63-64). If the flute player is prolific and going courting, flutes being used in the courting rituals of some tribes, his pack may contain items to purchase a wife (Martineau 1973:53). If he is associated with bringing warm weather or rain the pack may represent seeds for planting or harvested food. The flute player is also war medicine (Parsons 1966:381) and in the Hopi Flute Society that medicine gives power to dream coming events (ibid: 452). One of the Hopi female maidens is called Kokop'l Mana, or Humpback Maid, and appears both as a katchina and in dances (Wright 1979:110). The Hopi also associate Locust with the snake as both disappear in the fall as cold weather approaches and then reappear in the spring. Therefore, it is believed they aid in ending the cold weather (Titiev 1992:150). "The Locust bring warm weather, that is the reason why the priests often …throw pieces of a locust on the fireplace and burn it because the smoke and odor bring warm weather" (Voth 1905:220).

Locust brings warm weather by playing his flute as we see in the following story about the snakes: In the summer the Hopi were snakes and ran around in their snake skins. In the winter they stayed in their kiva, hung their snake skins on pegs and were Hopis again. One winter when the snow was very deep, they were running out of wood and many had already frozen to death. They decided to send one of their people to ask the locust for help. Racer was the only snake able to make it through the snow to the locust kiva. The locust were also transformed into Hopi when in their kiva in the wintertime. Because locust play flutes in their ceremonies their kiva was nice and warm and they had the finest of foods. They promised to help the Snake People in four days, and one went outside and blew his flute along the tracks of Racer melting the snow to clear his path back home. Four days later when the locust arrived at the Snake kiva, chirping through their flutes, it began to get warm and eventually the Snake People, the Hopi, were all sweating it was so hot. The locust returned home after singing a song, and in the morning when the Snake People went outdoors, all the snow had melted and only water remained. The Snakes sat in the sun and were not cold anymore (Voth 1905:217-220).

Locust "plays his flute on the Flute Society altar at Walpi" (Waters 1950:300) where we find it associated with clouds and rain (Parsons 1966: 704). We also find tiles of Flute People among the Hopi (Stephen 1936:Plate XXII) showing images with long appendages of some sort (ears, or perhaps wings) extending back from their bodies, and playing cone-shaped flutes. One figure has a convex chest that appears puffed out, and both are playing over what appear to be hills of corn and corn plants. These apparently depict Locust playing their flutes for warm weather, thus making the corn grow. The corn appears as connecting squares, or checkerboards containing a dot. Below each of the three "hills" pictured on the tile there are four larger squares each containing a dot in its center. These connecting squares may have a twofold meaning as the Zuni constructed "waffle gardens" in which to plant their crops. A 1911 photo is shown in Stars Above Earth Below (Bol 1998:120). These gardens are pictured as connecting squares, which look like the top of a waffle, which the women shaped "to retain water to nourish a variety of plants grown within them" (ibid:120). Bandelier observed these garden spaces in Sonora, Mexico, and Arizona and states "they appear to have been used to catch moisture, even dew, on the upland, or mountain slopes" (1975:407). The same type of spaces as described by Bandelier are located in the Mountainair area (author). They are almost always located near a ruin on a gentle slope, are rectangular in shape, and are formed by small stones protruding above ground level.

The connecting square design, each containing a dot, is pictured on ears of corn on a Pueblo ceremonial headdress (Miles 1973 :145), and also were painted on black-on-white southwestern pottery in New Mexico and Salado polychrome in Arizona (author).

Among the Zuni the Little Firebrand Society is described as playing flute-like trumpets made from a "long reed with a bell-shaped

FIGURE 3
Locust playing his flute over hills of corn

PETROGLYPH 17 - Flute player with blunderbuss

gourd at the tip" (Parsons 1966:380-381). It is played by the rain chief during rain ceremonies to call the clouds (ibid: 692, 739, 745); and as we will see in Chapter 8 it represented "Water serpent's dreadful voice" (ibid: 781). Some Keres flutes are described as having six holes and "a bell-shaped piece attached at the lower end, like a blunderbuss" (Curtis 1970 VOL. XVI: 127); the flutes used at the Jemez Flute Dance also have flaring tips (Parsons 1966: 684). The Mountainair Petroglyph 17 shows a figure with a convex chest and long ears. In one hand is a cone-shaped object, or flute, like those pictured on the Hopi Flute altar tile described above.

I observed one other flute player in the area with this type of flute while the others depicted are just a long line as in Petroglyph 16.

The Hopi also have Locust medicine, owned by the Flute Society, for curing wounds and for bringing true dreams (Parsons 1966:192).

As with other deities, we see the "humped back flute-player" adapting to different roles. When representing the insect Locust is important to various Pueblo groups in their emergence myth from the underworld. The Hopi believed that by playing his flute, Locust brought the warm weather and moisture in the spring making their crops grow. If fertile and carrying a back pack he may be associated with courting. We will see in Chapter 10 that the flute player may be connected to the Sandhill Crane Clan.

CHAPTER 7

Gods of the Prey

According to Zuni mythology six Prey Gods, or warriors, existed to guard the Father of the Medicine Societies in the City of Mists, or the middle place. These animals, also called Beast Gods, were: the mountain lion, bear, badger, eagle, wolf, and mole (Cushing 1994: 16). One of their places of origin was the Jemez Mountains (Ferguson 1985:23), 40 to 50 miles north of the present day city of Albuquerque; and another the Sandia Mountains (Dutton 1963:84), directly east of Albuquerque.

In the southwest, various stone images of these animals were kept on altars, among them the Altar of the Great Fire Fraternity (Stevenson 1904 PL CXVI) and the Altar of the Swordswallower Fraternity (Stevenson 1904 PL CVIII). Stone fetishes were also carried by travelers to act as guardians and "Prey animals are associated with war, particularly in the West and at Jemez" (Parsons 1966:186-188). Thus, it is these Beast Gods from which the Hunt Shaman reportedly received their power and the Zunis associated them with the east orienting their curing rites in that direction. Stone images of the Beast Gods, among other items, were kept in sacred bundles which the Zunis brought from the underworld with them (Sturtevant 1979:501). Cougar, Badger, Bear, Wolf, Eagle and Shrew are some of the Zuni Beast Gods that are believed to own certain plants or medicines (Stevenson 1915:37). The Keres origin legend associates

51

curing with the Cougar, Bear, Wolf, and Eagle (Curtis 1970 VOL. XVI: 173).

Stone images of these animals were thought to protect the households where they resided and if not properly cared for could bring harm. Thus offerings, including cornmeal, were made to them (Bunzel 1992:490-491,796). "From time immemorial, the Pueblo Indians have offered sacred cornmeal to their deities; indeed, so general is the custom even to this day that it may be said that there is no ceremony of which it does not form a part" (Hodge 1945:238). In Tewa mythology corn possesses a major role and "all aspects of the plant are considered symbolically powerful" (Sweet 1985:23). Corn and its uses has been examined in Chapter 5.

All six Beast Gods, or Gods of the Prey, are possibly represented in the area with the lion, eagle, wolf and mole definitely depicted. These will be discussed in this section. Evidence of all four has also been found outside of the Pueblo area.

Mountain Lion

The mountain lion, also called long-tail, is found both as a Pictograph (Chapter 2, Pictograph 1, Lion, page 14), as a Petroglyph (Chapter 3, Petroglyph 5, Two lions in Abo Pass, page 20); and in the form of stone effigies Image 1 and Figure 4. "T(t)he mountain lion is characterized by a long tail bent over the body of the quadruped" (Young 1988:156) while a decoration over a Zuni altar, where a lion represents the northwest, is shown with a long tail extending straight out from its body (ibid: 102-103). The north wall of the Hopi Warrior Society chamber had charcoal drawings of several beasts of prey including the mountain lion (Curtis 1970 VOL. XII-a: 133).

The Pawnee Indians of the southern plains considered the mountain lion one of the great powers of the heavens; and their sacred bundles, which possessed the animal powers, controlled disease and body health (Murie 1981:30, 45).

The mountain lion is found painted on shields of the Santo Domingo Indians (Wright 1976:40-41,71-73) and is believed to be a hunter of bison, deer, and elk

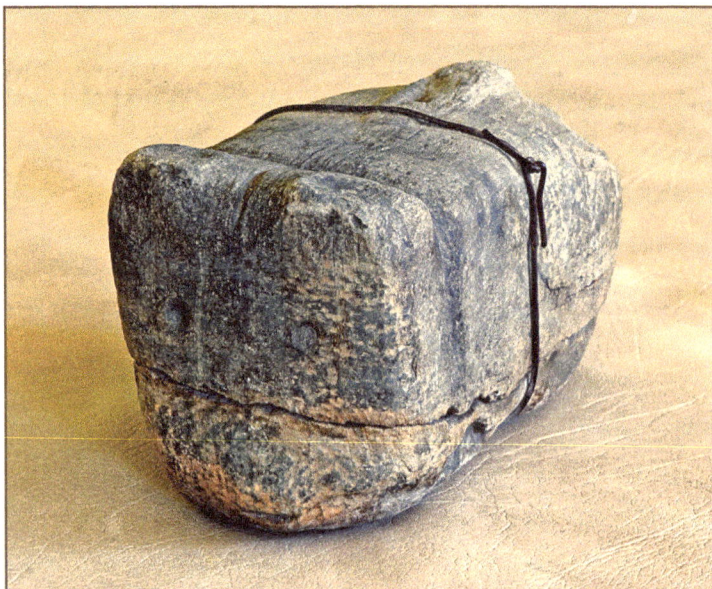

IMAGE 1 - Stone lion effigy

(Cushing 1994:31). The root of the aster, called lion medicine, was used to give strength to hunters (Parsons 1966:189). One of the most hazardous curing orders "magicanship" was possessed by the mountain lion and was able to suck objects causing illness from a patient, restore destroyed objects, and lift heavy items with feathers (Sturtevant 1979:505). The lion was a major Zuni Prey God fetish and master over all other Prey Gods, thus making it very highly prized (Cushing 1994:200). Mountain lion clans existed among many pueblo groups including the Tewa, the Keresan (Hodge 1912: 651,929), and the Hopi (Curtis 1970 VOL. XII-a: 74). At the Keresan Pueblo the Mountain Lion Clan, since it is a hunt society, was responsible for supplying meat for the Town Chief (Parson 1966:909). To aid in hunting some lion fetishes had red paint applied to their facial area and toes (Bandelier 1966:176) possibly representing blood.

A stone mountain lion effigy was recovered from a Salado site (A.D. 1100-1450) in the Tonto Basin in central Arizona. It was "nearly identical to fetishes still made and used by the Zuni people of New Mexico" (Rice 1993:3).

To the Pawnee the mountain lion symbolized the northwest (Murie 1981: 110), and to the Pueblos it also represents the direction north (Cushing 1994:201) or northwest (Young 1988:103) and usually the color yellow (Wright 1976:73; Young 1988:203). The yellow mountain lion is believed to be the older brother of other various colored lions (Cushing 1994:201). The lion in Pictograph 1 (Chapter 2, page 14) is painted primarily in yellow.

The two lions in Petroglyph 5 (Chapter 3, page 20) are looking down Abo Pass which leads to the Abo Pueblo and also to the salinas (salt beds) in the Estancia Valley which held major importance for the Indians. "The gathering of salt, a partly economic, partly religious ceremony" (Lange 1959:143) was a very important occasion. Trips, which were made on foot before the acquisition of the horse/ mule, sometimes taking over two weeks and covering a distance of almost 100 miles, were made from the Cochiti Pueblo to the salt beds. During this time strict taboos were observed, especially by the men who entered the lake to collect the salt (ibid: 142-143). Since the Beast Gods acted as protectors it is possible these animals "stand guard" in this spot in Abo Pass. Also, considering the human shape of the back leg of the larger lion and that they are wearing headdresses they possibly represent members of the Lion Clan.

The 1965-1967 excavation of Mound 7 at Grand Quivira National Monument (26 miles south of Mountainair) produced six mountain lion effigies. These are described as follows, "All six carry the raised tail on their backs, and all have full jaws that—partially as a result of short, stubby legs—almost reach the ground. The eye sockets are drilled, large, round and deep. While the erect ears have

IMAGE 2 - Train approaching Abo Pass from the west

been carefully carved, the mouths are indicated by a simple scratch" (Hayes 1981:133). Stone images may be "elaborately carved, others merely natural forms, slightly shaped" (Parsons 1966: 334).

A stone lion effigy, in Image 1 and in Figure 4, fitting the description of the ones recovered from Grand Quivira was found by Mr. R.L. Chilton on the Chilton ranch. Mr. Chilton's effigy, slightly bigger than the largest one from Grand Quivira measures approximately 10" long, between 4.5" and 5" high, 5" wide, and weighs 12 pounds. The lion has a raised area on its back depicting the tail, four slightly raised rectangular feet, small ears, drilled round eyes, and a single scratch for its mouth. The convex facial area has been ground smooth and there are round, smooth indentation on either side of the head above each ear. The lion has a wide groove around the head and across the bottom, possibly for bindings that attached objects. Cushing says of a mountain lion of yellow limestone, "An arrow-point of flint is bound to the back with cordage of cotton…" (1994:25), and of another, "there is cut around the neck a groove by which the beads of shell, coral, & c., were originally fastened" (1994:25). Fetishes are pictured in his report with various objects tied to them (Cushing 1994: PL I-V; PL V; PL VIII; PL X; PL XI), sometimes including a bag of cornmeal for food and they were believed to have had the "power to change into a living animal and actually run down the quarry" (Parsons1966:336).

Another lion effigy fitting the description of those found at Mound 7 at Grand Quivera National Monument was discovered by one of Mr. Chilton's neighbors (R.L. Chilton, personal communication 1993).

Fetishes, or stone images, of mountain lions were one of the objects on the Antelope Altar at Walpi in the late 1800s (Fewkes 1900:981), the Hopi Snake Kiva Altar (Curtis 1970 VOL. XII-a: 144), various Keres altars (Curtis 1970 VOL. XVI: 135; 149; 155, 160), and the Hunt Chief's Altar at San Felipe (Parsons 1966: 834). The Keres also used stone mountain lions in burial ceremonies, healing ceremonies, and as protection against sorcerers (Curtis 1970 VOL. XVI:82-3;99;119). The Cochiti Indians had shrines that consisted of pairs of stone lions. One pair, located in Bandelier National Monument, is still visited by Cochiti hunters today (Lange 1959: Plate 3; Plate 4). A pair of natural size crouching mountain lions was also reported by Bandelier in the Cochiti area (Bandelier 1966: 169). This is probably the pair the Zuni Indians believe stand guard at a sacred spot of theirs, their place of origin, which is also an old hunters shrine, near the Pueblo of Cochiti (Dutton 1963:206). Whether the Zunis lions and the ones observed by Bandelier are one of the pair pictured by Lange is unclear.

Although the mountain lion is master over all other Prey Gods, Coyote, in the Order of the Hunt is given for "traditional reasons higher sacred rank than the mountain lion" (Cushing 1994:30-31). The Hopi hunt chief used prayer feathers with a lion fetish and then the coyote, associated with kills, would be listened for. If the coyote was heard it meant that it was chasing the deer and the deer would "be tired the next day and easy to kill" (Parsons: 1966:447). This placement of these two fetishes mark them as the most important.

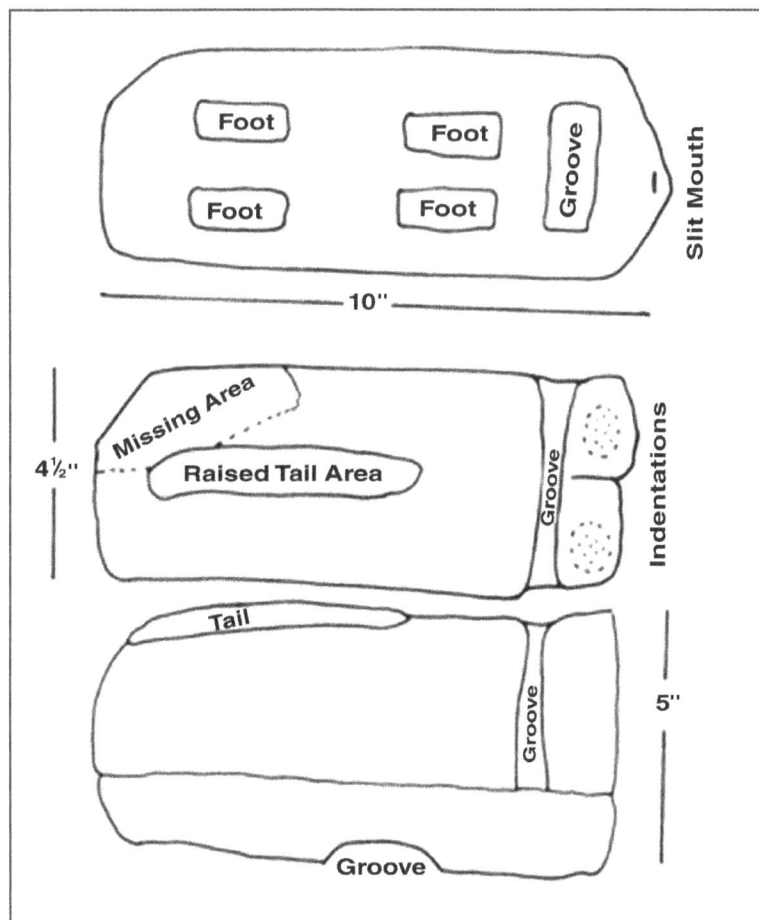

Mountain lion effigy - FIGURE 4

Wolf/Coyote

Wolf, hunter of the east, is "characterized by erect attitudes, usually oblique faces, pricked-up ears, and "hanging tails." Fetishes existed in yellow (north), blue (west), white (east), red (south), many-colored (upper regions), and black (nadir), some being stained with red pigment (Cushing 1994:28). Coyote is described the same except with a horizontal or slightly drooping tail (ibid:26).

Navajo sandpaintings from the Coyote Chant (Luckert 1979:228) pictures coyote preciously as described above and as shown in Mountainair Petroglyph 18. After the Spanish revolt of 1680 some of the Pueblo people that fled the Rio Grande area were absorbed by the Navajo thus accounting for shared traditions and mythology concerning coyote. The Navajo name used for the coyote is the same name used for the wolf (ibid: 4-8), thus coyote and wolf may be interchangeable.

A Wolf Clan existed among the Pueblo Indians and was the war god from which the hunt shaman received their powers and taught the Zuni their hunting rituals (Parsons: 1996:359,184,187-188). The staining of red pigment on fetishes perhaps indicated blood and a successful hunt. However, since coyote was thought to call disease, the Zuni did not want the wolf/coyote living too close to them so distributed prayer feathers in the four directions making the coyote and wolf live off in the hills (ibid: 271).

Another role of coyote was to call the rain in the day (Luckert 1979:228) and at night to call sickness, thus introducing death (Parsons 1996: 193-94). The sketch of the Agricultural panel (Chapter 13, Figure 7, pages 100, 101) shows coyote on the far right with his mouth open as if he is calling. His tail is raised and directly above it is a figure associated with a plant. This panel contains many agricultural symbols so this many depict coyote calling the rain for the crops and wild plants.

PETROGLYPH 18 - Wolf/coyote

Eagle

Many petroglyphs of birds resembling eagles are located in the area. Some have hooked beaks, outspread wings, and extended legs showing feet with exposed claws, as seen in Petroglyph 19. Sometimes only the profile of a head is present, Petroglyph 20. This latter petroglyph, which may relate to a ceremony discussed in the following chapter, shows the outline of a head that is almost identical to an eagle mask used by the Kwakiutl Indians of British Columbia (Mallery 1972:696). One pictograph of an eagle is painted white with red stripes. The eagle represents the God of the Upper Regions with the white eagle representing the eastern skies (Cushing 1994:29).

Among the Indians of the southwest reported to have Eagle Clans are the Zuni and the Hopi (Hodge 1912:744, 749). A carved eagle fetish resembling figures illustrated in "Zuni Fetishes" (Cushing 1994: Plate VIII, numbers 3 & 6) was recovered from the same Salado area in central Arizona as the mountain lion effigy mentioned previously (author). It was fashioned from dark stone and was somewhat teardrop shaped with a deep groove on either end and another in the

Eagles - PETROGLYPH 19

PETROGLYPH 20
Snake with circle and eagle head

shape of an X crossing its back. Eagle wings on fetishes are described as "deep lines which cross over the back…" (Cushing 1994:29), exactly like the one from Arizona. Pictograph 12, on the vertical face of the sandstone, depicts an eagle painted in red with crosses, or lines, that X over the back .

A Zuni story (Bunzell 1973:864-867) tells of a lost boy who is rescued by an eagle and given some of its sacred feathers. The boy's father decides the eagle feathers would be worn by the katchinas since the eagle flies up so high above the pollution of the world. Thus, the eagle and its feathers are associated with a clean, pure heart and seeing in all directions and is prayed to for good health. Most of the bird symbols representing eagles are located high on the stone outcrops positioning them higher (in the air) than the other associated symbols, such as the ones in Petroglyph 19.

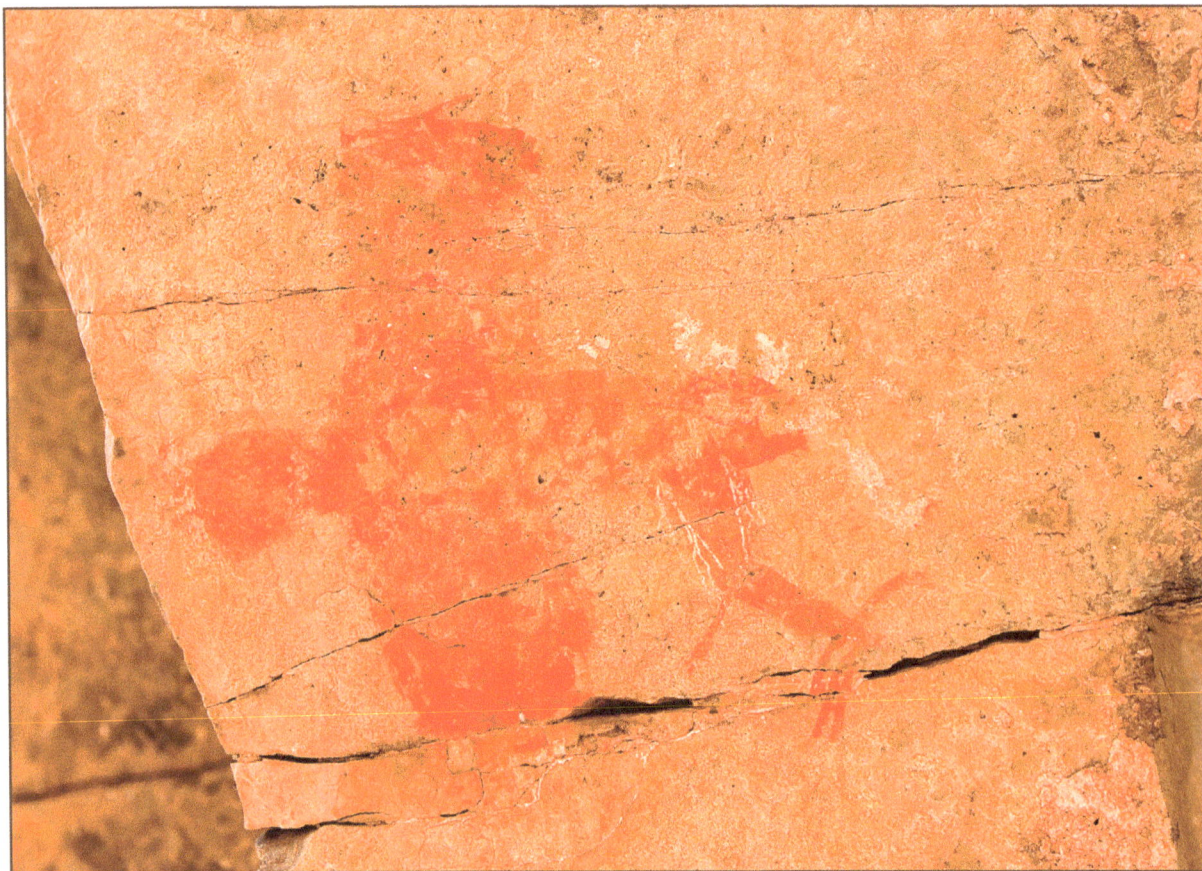

PICTOGRAPH 12 - Eagle with XX's on its Back

Mole

The mole, who is God of the Lower regions, appears to have been in less demand due to its size and not being as mighty as the other Prey Gods. However, "from the fact that it is able by burrowing to lay traps for the largest game of earth…"(Cushing 1994:30) is considered important.

Mole Clans existed among the Hopi and Isleta Indians in the southwest (Hodge 1912:299, 964). In Hopi mythology Mole assisted in the destruction of both the Winged Snake and the Bird Monster (Curtis 1970 VOL. XII-a:195-197, 212).

In the initiation ceremony into the Shaman Society the Keres Indians prayed to the spirit helper Mole asking that the young initiative "have strength and long life and come safely through to the time of his initiation" (Curtis 1970 VOL. XVI: 89). Songs during the ceremony also asked Mole to put the power in the young man's heart that he had in his so he could do what Mole, and the other spirit helpers, including the cougar and eagle, did (ibid: 89,91). Mole was also called upon by the Keres to help cure individuals in purification rites (ibid: 117-119).

In Mexico the mole appears in legends by aiding Quetzalcoatl, the feathered serpent, in the underworld search for his father's bones (Nicholson 1985:91).

Petroglyph 4 (Chapter 3, Prey mole, page 19) shows a mole portrayed by its long snout, short ears, a tiny eye, humped back, and long tail. The symbol has its small body in a curved position that represents digging or burrowing and is located in a recessed area in the rock that may indicate hidden or underground. This is where one would find a mole since they live in the dark "underworld." This panel is visible only by walking on the uphill side of the slope and looking down into the opening in the boulder. Cushing (1994: 30) states that fetishes of the mole are very rare and illustrates one (Plate III, figure 5) with the same tiny eye, ear, and long nose.

Thus, each of the Beast Gods, or Gods of the Prey, discussed above has its own special powers which are symbolic of attributes it possesses. When praying to one of these gods it was not the effigy itself that is appealed to but the characteristics or powers it represented.

The mountain lion, ranked first among the Prey Gods, was a powerful hunter of the larger game animals, and was prayed to by war chiefs for power and for a good hunt. Its picture appeared on shields and lion medicine was used for hunting strength. The mountain lion was also recognized as a guardian.

Ranked next to mountain lion in importance is wolf/coyote. The Navajo name for coyote and wolf is interchangeable and due to contact between the Navajo and Pueblo Indians they shared common mythology concerning the two. The Wolf Clan gave the hunt shaman his powers and taught the Zuni their hunting rituals. Coyote also was responsible for calling the rain so may be associated with agriculture.

The eagle, possessing good eyesight and having the ability to fly up high in the clean pure air, represented having a pure heart as well as the ability to see great distances. The eagle feather is respected and powerful, or sacred, and is used by katchinas and Native Americans on dance regalia at pow wows and ceremonies. Among some tribes, the eagle feather must never touch the ground and if this accidentally happens a qualified person must pray over the feather to bless it before it is touched or picked up.

Mole was smaller in size but never the less an important god. Due to the size and digging ability it could burrow underground and lay traps for larger unsuspecting animals. It was also important in initiation and curing ceremonies. Few mole fetishes were made and are quiet rare.

A few petroglyphs in the Mountainair region may represent the badger, and/or the bear (Image 3).

Images of all Beast Gods were considered guardians and carried by travelers for protection and good luck. Many of the fetishes were used on ceremonial altars and some Indian groups outside of the southwest also had them.

IMAGE 3 - Possible badger or bear

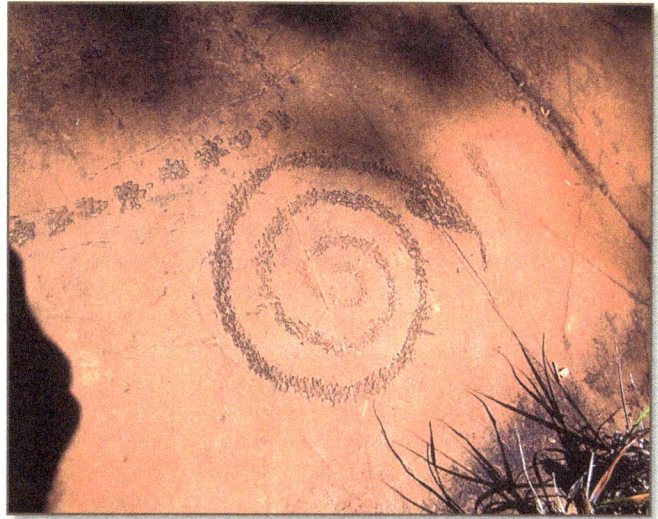

The Snake or Serpent

One of the most common symbols in the Mountainair area is the snake, or serpent. This symbol is found isolated, in groups of two or more, or with other symbols. The form may be coiled or zigzagged, with or without rattles, and/or a 'horn' on its head. It may appear as either a petroglyph or a pictograph. Petroglyph 21 shows a small panel of three snakes, one coiled and two in a zigzag form. The one on the left has a horn on its head while the one on the right has rattles (crosses) on the tail. Two of the serpents have triangular, or arrow-shaped heads, which may relate to the action of striking.

The Zunis had many fetishes of snakes and some were considered to have even greater power than the Prey Gods (Tyler 1964: 227) discussed in Chapter 7. When studying philosophy relating to Zuni fetishes Frank Cushing states that any object or occurrence observed in nature was believed to possess a personality closest to the animal whose actions it favored. "Lightning is often given the form of a serpent, with or without an arrow-pointed tongue, because its course through the sky is serpentine, its stroke instantaneous and destructive; yet it is named Wi-lo-lo-a-ne, a word derived not from the name of the serpent itself, but from that of its most obvious trait, its gliding, zigzag motion" (Cushing 1979:195). Among the Hopi "the similarity between the sinuous gliding of a snake and the broken

PETROGLYPH 21 - Three snakes

course of a lightning flash came naturally the concept of serpents as messengers of the rain deities" (Curtis 1970 VOL. XII-a: 155).

Due to their zigzag course and striking power the snake is associated with lightning which brings rain and fertility to the land which in turn brings crops. When the figure of a snake has been portrayed "the serpent is no snake, but stands for sheet-lightning" (Bandelier 1966: 207) and during the Walpi Snake Ceremony both snakes and lightning are portrayed by the same zigzag symbol (Tyler:1964: 226-229).

The snake is found among many indigenous peoples including the Southwestern Pueblos Indians and farther to the south the Aztecs and Toltecs. It may symbolize either good or bad and some tribes considered it immortal because of the shedding of the skin which is looked upon as a rebirth, or of living again and again.

When captive snakes were used in Pueblo ceremonies and released they returned to the underworld, where some tribes believe lies a system of rivers and lakes to which they convey their messages. After all, springs emerge up out of the earth, as does the snake, so the Horned Water Serpent is believed to be god of these waters (Tyler 1964: 229, 234). This association is also seen at Zuni where the Rain Chief is in charge of the Water Serpent (Parsons 1966: 877).

Snake Clans were found among various tribes including the Zunis, Hopis, and Keres (Tyler 1964: 229). As far back as 1583 a ceremony was witnessed at Acoma using live snakes which were kept in captivity by the Indians (Curtis 1970 VOL. XVI: 209, 245). The Hopi believe their first people were Snake People (refer to page 48 and the story about the Hopi and snakes) with the Water Serpent being the patron of their Water Corn Clan (Waters 1950: 316). At Hopi the task of the head person of the Rattlesnake Clan was to cleanse "any place that has been struck by lightning" (Curtis 1970 VOL. XII-a: 156). The Tewa Indians, composing five villages in the Rio Grande Valley north of Santa Fe, possessed a complex snake cult, the knowledge of which they guarded with their lives.

Snake dances, or the handing of live snakes, may also have taken place in the Mountainair area as Bandelier (1975: 79) recorded in the 1880s that the Abo Painted Rocks site had a painting of a black and white "Qo-sha-re" (ceremonial figure) handling a snake. Cole (1984: 9) reports the photograph of a 1932 drawing showing a Koshare (or Qu-sha-re), superimposed by a snake, stepping from a pot and states that it fits Bandelier's earlier description. When the site was visited in 1993 the very faded fragment of a black and white image of a person and the partial image of snake to its right was located. Deteriorating symbols had their heads missing and the pot from which the Koshare was stepping could not be distinguished. The snake had been painted in white with red dots and a yellow ochre tail. Pictograph 13 was taken of one painting in 2005 and shows the faded but recognizable white snake, which is outlined in a solid white, with bands above the yellow rattles on its tail (center far left). To the right of the snake appears a masked figure, different than the one referred to by Cole in her report.

Legends exist among some Southwestern Indians of very large or giant snakes. In Hopi mythology when hunters were disappearing in the mountains Great Rattlesnake assisted the people by destroying the culprit, "winged-snake" (Curtis 1970 VOL. XIII-a: 195-197). In the Hopi Reed Clan migration story the huge snake, Katoya, guarded the Snake Rock of the Rattlesnake Clan, called Tuqi, which translates to "mountain" (ibid: 91,109). The Sandia, Isleta, and San Juan Indians were also reported to have had very large or monstrous snakes to which they fed rabbits and cornmeal (Bandelier 1975: 111; 277).

Another legend concerning a giant snake and a sacred mountain in Nevada is shared by most of the Yuman speaking tribes, among them the Hualapai of northern Arizona. This story is particularly interesting as it includes both a pictograph in La Cueva de la Serpiente

PICTOGRAPH 13 - Snake and ceremonial figure

(Cave of the Serpent) in Arroyo del Parral located in the Sierra de San Francisco in Baja, California, and a story about Spirit Mountain, Nevada. The following information is from a personal communication (LaVan Martineau 1996), "The Legacy of the Giants"(Martineau Video Productions:1996), and my visit to both of these areas. The story of the giant snake itself is fascinating since the Baja pictograph is one of the "Great Murals" that is believed to have been painted by a race of Giants from the north, who invaded the residents of that area, the Cochimi. The Giants were eventually expelled because the Cochimi could not allow such people in their land. This legend of the Giants was recorded by Jesuit missionaries of that area in the mid 1700s and is attributed both to very large human bones they saw and to the huge pictographs, many of which were painted overhead on rock surfaces in caves or shelters. Some of the pictograph shelters visited had ceilings that were at least 30 feet above the ground and completely covered with larger than life figures. Our guides, and the residents of that area, still attribute these paintings to the reported race of Giants. In The Cave of the Serpent the main figure is a snake approximately twelve feet long with smaller human figures and several animals standing on either side of it. In the story, this large snake, which was made by the Creator, traveled north by sea and then overland to Spirit Mountain, Nevada, where it was killed and turned to stone.

A large natural rock formation in the shape of a giant snake, Image 4, is located outside of Laughlin, near Spirit Mountain. The rocks form a giant rattlesnake with a triangular-shaped head with a flat nose, the body and then a raised tail with two rattles. Is it possible this natural formation represents the giant snake in that Yuman legend, the same one painted in the Cave of the Serpent in Baja, California? The Native Americans that inhabited the Spirit

Natural rock formation in the shape of a giant snake - IMAGE 4

Mountain region were aware of this rock formation as surface sites and a large petroglyph panel are located in the immediate area.

Near Nambe Falls, New Mexico, the Tewa Indians say "are natural rock formations resembling two large serpents (some people claim there is only one) to which have been ascribed supernatural powers" (Sweet 1985: 55). The Snake Society of the Sia (Zia) has enormous carvings of coiled snakes beside its Rain Altars (Parsons 1966: 687-688).

The Hohokam Indians of Arizona carved rattlesnake ornaments from shell and also decorated carved stone bowls with snakes (Tanner 1976:173, 204-206). Rattlesnake images were found at Pueblo Bonito in Chaco Canyon, New Mexico, as well as in Hopi country as effigies (Tyler 1964: 226, 227), and painted on Salado pottery (circa 1250 to 1450) in central Arizona (author). The Zunis had

PETROGLYPH 22 - Snake cane

snake or horned serpent fetishes which were owned by the North Priest and were used to treat sicknesses or snakebite and sometimes to control the weather (Tyler 1964:227).

Petroglyph 22 shows a snake-shaped cane from the Mountainair area representing a water serpent. On the end of the handle is the head; next the zigzag body which may relate to lightning, and/or rain; and the tip of the cane is the tail. Canes represent status or power and the Hopi Indians carved their canes in the shape of a water serpent (Waters 1950:369). This symbol was also discussed in Chapter 5.

Several Mountainair petroglyphs show a serpent rising up out of a circle one of which appears to relate to the production of rainfall and may be seen in Petroglyph 20 (Chapter 7, page 58). The serpent is zigzagged to show movement and the triangular head indicates striking. J. Walter Fewkes in his report to the Smithsonian Institution on "SUN WORSHIP OF THE HOPI INDIANS" (1920: 493-526) investigates ceremonies pertaining to crop production. The Hopis had no means of irrigation for corn, their main food source, and relied upon moisture from the sky. Without rain they would have no crops and the power that brought it was considered supernatural. Prehistoric peoples had no scientific understanding of weather patterns and depended on ceremonies and symbolism handed down from past generations to produce needed rainfall. Sun Worship rites were not only to "draw back the sun" when the solstice occurred, but to bring new life and fertility to the earth. The ceremonies included, among other things, a horned serpent that symbolized the Sky God and rain, and a Bird God that represented the sun. At Walpi the horned serpent was not always present in these rites but the Bird God always played a major role. The Sky God is described as "wearing on his head a star with four points, the 'heart' of the sky." The four points perhaps represent the four cardinal directions. Fewkes goes into great detail explaining the Hopi ceremonies that produced the needed rainfall which included serpent effigies emerging both from behind screens and out of jars. These sacred ceremonies took place in the kivas and were associated with the equinox. One of these reenactments is shown on Plate 5 of Fewkes' report and is acted out at the vernal (spring) equinox by the Hopi. He reported that two snakes emerged from pots with each pot having a four-pointed star painted on it to represent the Sky God. Petroglyph 20 (Chapter 7,

Snake with circle and eagle head, page 58) shows a snake rising out of a circle (a vessel) in a zigzag, or striking motion. On the panel, directly to the right of the snake, is a large bird head, Bird God. This symbol is the same as the Eagle Sun Mask of the Kwakiutl Indians (see the section on eagles, Chapter 7). Both the mask and petroglyph have a large hooked beak and open mouth. Fewkes says that in the ceremony the snake effigies swayed back and forth, over corn symbols before the pots, then struck at each other finally sinking back into their vessels. This is a ceremony with the snakes emerging from the earth, symbolic of water and perhaps a flood, sweeping over the cornfield, then returning back into the vessel, or the earth from where they emerged. During some ceremonies a gourd trumpet was blown to represent "Water Serpent's dreadful voice" (Parsons 1966: 781).

The Kiva mural paintings at Kuaua, New Mexico (Dutton 1963: Pl.XVI; Pl.XXII), contain symbols very much like the ones in Petroglyph 20. The murals show vessels, or pots, from which zigzag lines with triangular tips emerge and in two cases eagles are present with one painting showing the eagle directly over the vessel and lighting symbols and small dots (rain?) falling from its beak. Plate XVI is named "A depiction of the Universe" and Plate XXII is "Autum ceremony for fructification." The eagles, which live in the heavens, symbolizes messengers from the Above bringing rain to earth so the corn will grow and all people will have food (ibid: 128, 136). Thus, we see the Sun Worship of the Hopi Indians, the kiva murals at Kuaua, and the panel in Petroglyph 20 all containing the same symbols which are associated with the eagle, lightning, and rainfall for crop production.

In the Hopi migration story the Water Bullsnake, or horned serpent, was responsible for a disastrous flood which caused the Hopi to continue on their way north from their stop west of San Carlos, Arizona, on the Gila River (Curtis 1970 VOL. XII-a: 19). They say their Water Serpent came from the Red Land to the south (Parsons1966:184) and the horned serpent myth still exists among the Pima and Papago Indians of Arizona. The (horned) snake represents the Sun God, Tcuhu (Montezuma) who created channels, or irrigation ditches, with part of the river becoming a great serpent. Today Indians along the Gila River in Arizona still offer sacrifices to the irrigation ditches and worship the river (Fewkes 1920: 505).

As we have seen, the snake, or serpent, can be either beneficial or destructive and can also be associated with Mexico, where it is known as Quetzalcoatl. "Quetzalcoatl symbolizes the same concept as the plumed serpent of the Hopi…the male fructifying power of nature…" (Fewkes 1920: 511). A horned and feathered (plumed) serpent found among the murals painted at Pottery Mound near

Albuquerque, is shown with teeth and "consumes a purple man" (Hibben 1975: 58-59; Fig. 42).

Pictograph 6 (Chapter 3, page 22) shows the head of a horned feathered serpent painted black with a headdress of turquoise, gold, and red feathers and a turquoise horn. It has a white eye, white teeth, and an extended red tongue that is wrapped around what appears to be a spruce branch. Below the object in the mouth of the effigy is a clearer painting in dark green (not pictured) of what resembles the top of a fir or spruce tree with single needles. All spruce and firs have a single, fairly straight needle, as opposed to pines which, with the exception of the Singleleaf pinion, or pine, have curved needles grouped in two, threes or fives (Elmore 1976: 189).

Palolokon, the plumed or water serpent of the Hopi, also has a black head, white eyes, white teeth, a red projecting tongue, a feathered headdress, and a short curved horn (Fewkes 1920: 504; Branson 1992: 199). Also spelled Pa-lolokanu "water bull snake," whose home is said to be the spring Tawa-pa, is found in the February and March Hopi katchina dances, at times in their winter solstice ceremony (Curtis 1970 VOL. XII-a: 104-105), and in the spring solstice ceremony, as discussed above. As we saw in Chapter 2, black can be associated with the underworld and/or death, so is it possible this painting represents the plumed water serpent of the Hopi withholding its life giving rains from the plant life or nature. In other words, devouring, or holding back plants (represented by its tongue wrapped around the spruce limb) by not producing the life-giving rains. Or, the exact opposite may be true. The growth may represent food being swallowed as a result of moisture brought by the rainmakers (Martineau: personal communication 1999).

The spruce, used in numerous katchina dances, and representing moisture, is also important in the Hano emergence myth. Bear Old Man's Ladder, which he used to bring people up from the Lake of Emergence, was made of spruce. During some katchina ceremonies small spruce trees are planted and after the dances they are made into ladders for homes (Parsons 1966: 918,773, 785). The Cochiti also believe the spruce to be the tree their people climbed in their emergence story (Lange 1959: 348). Today spruce "are still collected with reverence because they remain powerful symbols of life" (Sweet 1985: 17). The spruce tree represents north to the Zuni (Stevenson 1904: 444-445), as well as the Hopi and is the direction from which the winter rains come (Tyler 1964: 251). In a February Tiwa ceremony dancers wear Douglas spruce to bring moisture in the form of snow for crop irrigation (Curtis 1970 VOL. XVI: 24), and "The breath from the gods of the undermost world is supposed to ascend through the trunks of these trees and form clouds behind which the rain-makers work" (Stevenson 1915: 97). Thus, the spruce "symbolizes all the green growing things with which the rain clothes the earth" (Bunzel 1973: 862), and the color blue-green "is said to represent the supreme, universal being" (Dutton 1963: 146). Along with being the color of the spruce, blue-green is also the color of the horn on Palolokon. Both the spruce and the Horned Serpent are sacred or supreme to the Pueblo Indians.

Many of the American Indian groups, including cultures from Mexico, have legends and prophesies foretelling the end of the world due to drought and starvation. If this proves true, then the great feathered serpent, which is responsible for water and the production of food, may also be responsible for destroying it by withholding the life giving waters.

The coiled snake found in the Mountainair area is also associated with a four pointed star that has a face, legs, and feet, Petroglyph 23. This snake may represent lightning, servant of the Sky God (Fewkes 1920: 507), who wore a four-pointed star on his head (ibid: 501) and is discussed in the following section on stars.

Coiled snake and star figure - PETROGLYPH 23

CHAPTER 9

Stars and Solar Panels

Located in the Mountainair area are a number of star symbols. Some of these are on shield figures, some associated with snakes and other figures, while some appear to be bodies with faces, legs, and feet. One of the latter, Petroglyph 24, is wearing the same type of crown or headdress that also appears on some animals and human figures. The crown is also seen on a star on the large panel of Petroglyph 3 (Chapter 2, page 16), lower and left of center. All stars I have observed, with one exception, have four points.

"Probably all stars, the Galaxy and the entire starry heaven, have an anthropomorphic divine character to the Pueblos" (Parsons 1966: 182). The Sun was prayed to for a long life, good luck in hunting, and power in war. Some events, such as eclipses, were feared and believed to have had the power to cause pregnant women to miscarry and even to kill (ibid:180-181).

One Mountainair panel contains three stars, an inverted crescent (possibly a moon), two snakes and other symbols. Only the star with the crescent above it are pictured in various texts and is sometimes referred to as a supernova. The crescent symbol is reported to be rare on panels and when found in close association with a bright object (star or planet) is assumed to be a supernova in the Crab-Nebula dating A.D.1054 (Brandt 1977:175). This may apply to the star and crescent mentioned above. However, no explanation was offered for

PETROGLYPH 24 - Star figure with headdress

the rest of the symbols on the panel. A crescent is also located to the left of the star and crown in Petroglyph 3.

The Mountainair panel of Petroglyph 25, Figure 5, appears to include Cassiopeia and Polaris among other symbols of a full circle, a crescent, a 4-pointed star, a number of other small dots, and one arrow with fletching and an arrow point. Southwestern people were not the only ones who recognized the W-shaped star group of Cassiopeia. Beside the Hopi and Navajo, the Maricopa/Pima of Arizona, and groups of the Arctic, Pacific Northwest, California, and the Great Plains also recognized this constellation. The Zunis called it Star Zigzag (Miller 1997:287-288). To help verify the importance of Cassiopeia and Polaris an explanation of the night-sky portion of a Navajo sand painting is helpful (Griffin-Pierce1992:116-128). Page 117 of that article shows a sketch of the sand painting with Cassiopeia, Polaris with the Big Dipper included. The article states that the two constellations are "the cornerstone and backbone of the Navajo ritual," which is part of the Blessingway Ceremony and concentrates on maintaining "order, harmony, balance, and peace necessary for the continuation and orderly functioning of the universe" (ibid:119). Without this harmony in nature and ones own life "there will be all kinds of misfortune in the world" (ibid:124). The article makes very clear the importance of the stars and their impact on rituals and belief. The American Indian closely watched the heavens and recognized the fact that Polaris, the north star, was the only light in the night sky that did not move. It's around Polaris that Cassiopeia and the Big Dipper revolve.

For centuries civilizations have easily recognized Cassiopeia by its W or M shape which appears as far back as 4,000 years ago in the Euphrates Valley on seals (Chartrand III 1982: 128). In "1572 one of the most important astronomical events in history occurred in Cassiopeia: a 'new star' appeared" (ibid:108). This supernova would have been visible by the residents of Southwest and was bright enough to have been seen by the naked eye. Petroglyph 25 may have recorded this event.

When examining this panel we see in the upper right corner the W-shape of Cassiopeia with a large four pointed star directly above it, Figure 5. Located farther to the north in the night sky are Polaris and other stars in the Big Dipper. Along with the star cluster of Cassiopeia, the panel contains a crescent, to the upper left an arrow with fletching and a point, another four pointed star and a full circle. The arrow appears out of place in a solar panel but among the Hopi

Solar panel - PETROGLYPH 25

**Symbols from Panel Possibly Recording
Supernova in Cassiopeia**

● **Star Cluster**

W-shaped Constellation of Cassiopeia

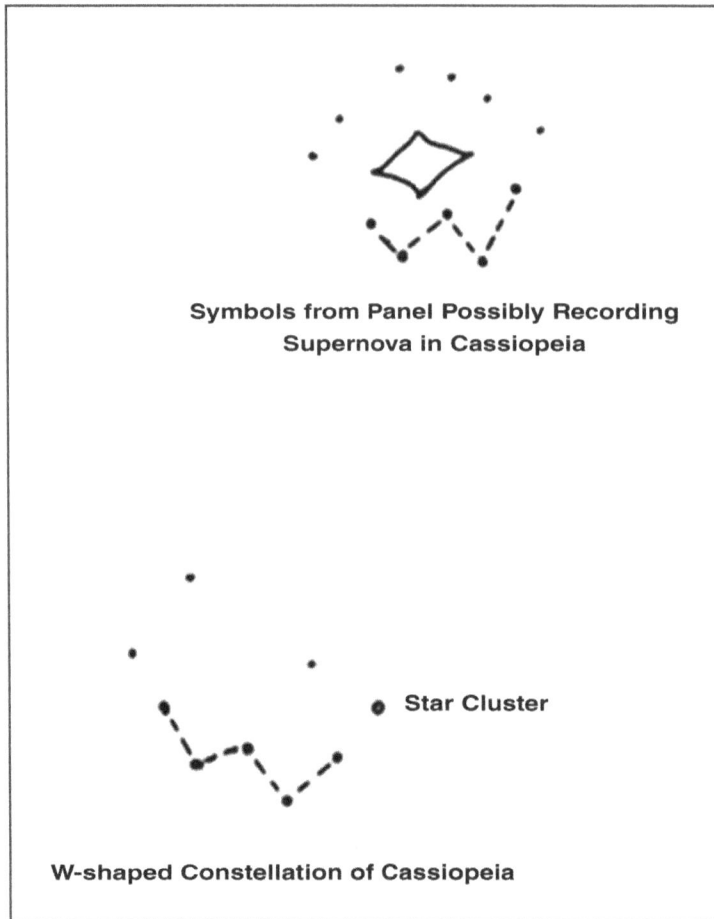

FIGURE 5 - Solar panel

the starry war god Sho'tokunungwa "is Lightning shooting arrow points from his fingertips..." (Parsons 1966:181). This may represent that god and helps explain an arrow on a solar panel. What better way to indicate arrow points being shot in the sky, or something that flashes through, or in, the sky, than by showing an arrow. Thus, the star directly to the left of the arrow may mean it is a star that is flashing. The two other symbols are the crescent and a circle. The crescent may represent dark, as a crescent moon gives off almost no light as opposed to the full moon or the sun (the full circle), which produces light. These symbols may indicate darkness and then the brightness, or light caused by the supernova which occurred in 1572. The supernova that did take place in the W-shaped formation of Cassiopeia produced a point of brightness which was visible to the residents of the Mountainair area. It is probable they observed this event and believed it of major importance to record.

A number of cultures studied the heavens and recorded events they observed. The Pawnee had a sky chart drawn on a piece of buckskin and were aware that Polaris was the only star in the sky that did not move (Chamberlain 1982:178, 187-205). Both the Pawnee and their relatives, the Wichita, had corn planting ceremonies (Dorsey 1904: 4) that were associated with Venus, known to them as Evening Star (Murie 1981:39). These ceremonies, like the previously mentioned Sun Worship rituals of the Hopi, were performed yearly to insure crop production (Chamberlain 1982:52-55). A bison scapula hoe with an engraved star and other planting symbols was recovered from a Wichita site in southern Kansas in 1995. The symbols on the artifact were related to Evening Star, her Sacred Garden, and the annual planting ceremonies and mythology of the Caddo Indians (Holland 1998), the linguistic descent of both the Wichita and Pawnee.

The largest star shield figure located in the Mountainair area is on the vertical face of a rectangular slab of sandstone which makes the figure appear to be lying on its side. There has been a small amount of exfoliation of the rock surface; hence the figure is not 100% complete. Also, lichen is growing on the feet, legs and lower part of the shield. The symbol, Petroglyph 2 (Chapter 2, page 13), Figure 6, is larger than most petroglyph symbols in the area. A large star is located in the center of the shield and nine triangular points radiate out from the head, a small portion of which is missing. On the same rock slab near the figures head are two more four-pointed stars, one quite large and the second one smaller. The smaller of the two is shown at the very beginning of this chapter.

Petroglyph 23 (Chapter 8, Coiled snake and star figure, page 69) shows one of the star figures with a face, legs and feet. To its left is located a coiled snake which we have seen may represent lightning, and/or to strike. This may represent the Star God, or War God, also a Lightning God referred to above as Sho'tokunungwa (Tyler 1964: 98). In one of the Sun Worship Ceremonies of the Hopi the snake represents lightning, the servant of the Sky God (Fewkes 1920: 507). A diorama circa 1900 from a Soyal, or solstice, ritual at Oribi on the Hopi mesa shows a man wearing a four-pointed star shaped headdress/mask (Brody 1991: Plate 39). This "heart" of the sky, or Sky God, with the four-pointed star on his head, symbolizes both the horned serpent and the sun. The sun gives warmth for the crops to grow and the serpent brings the rain to water the soil (Fewkes 1920: 501) both necessary for crop production.

Among the Hopi "...the Sky, or Star God, was prayed to in the old ritual. We recall that the War chief has a star effigy on his altar..." (Stephen 1936:84). The Star God was above all else a war god and the name means "heart of the above" or "heart of the stars" (Tyler 1964: 98-99).

An Anasazi Pottery Mound kiva mural shows stars with four points and faces called "spirit figures" and "soul faces." Some of these are wearing feathered headdresses, similar to the Mountainair symbol in Petroglyph 24, and two are associated with rattlesnakes (Hibben 1975:48,134-134). A kiva painting at Jemez depicting the universe shows the Morning Star and Evening Star both with four points and faces (Brody 1991: 146).

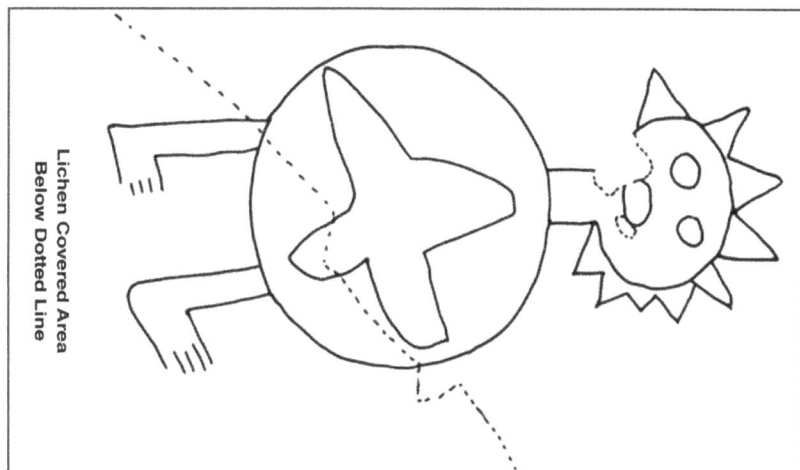

Large star shield figure - FIGURE 6

Stars with eight points appear more rare with only one being located in the area, Petroglyph 26, far right. An almost identical eight-pointed star design was woven into a Paiute basket made around 1920-1930. The star is said to be of Washoe influence (Wade 1986:76); the Washoe were a tribe living in California and Nevada who were conquered by the Paiutes (Swanton 1984:383-384). An eight-pointed star appears on the Hopi Soyal mask of Pawikkatcina (Fewkes 1990: 300). A more elaborate eight-pointed symbol with a highly stylized bird in its center is considered a sun symbol and combines both the sun, having eight points, and a bird called a Sky God symbol (Fewkes 1973:158). Although the shapes are different, we see the same type of symbolism in referring back to the Sun Worship of the Hopi Indians (previous section) where this combination of symbols represented by the Eagle Sun Mask, whose shape is the same as the Bird God in association with the vessels, signified the Sky God, renewer of life, with a snake emerging from it. Petroglyph 20 (Chapter 7, Snake with circle and eagle head, page 58) which shows a circle or pot, does not have a star on it, as Fewkes shows, but to the right of the panel is a "shield figure" with a four-pointed star on its shield. From the flexed position of the legs it is running and is facing, or going, in the direction of the bird head and the snake rising from the circle. The star is the same as the ones on the vessels in the solstice ceremony. "Running occurs in many ceremonials…to assist the movement of Sun and Moon, to speed up the clouds, or to hasten the growth of crops" (Parsons 1966:393). This runner with a star shield may be hastening the production of rain and warmth to speed up crop growth.

The Mountainair region shows the four-pointed star used in different ways. It may be associated with shield figures, solar panels, the sun mask and the snake. The star may represent, among other things, the Star God, War God, and Lightning God and perhaps even more important, crop production.

PETROGLYPH 26 - Eight-pointed star

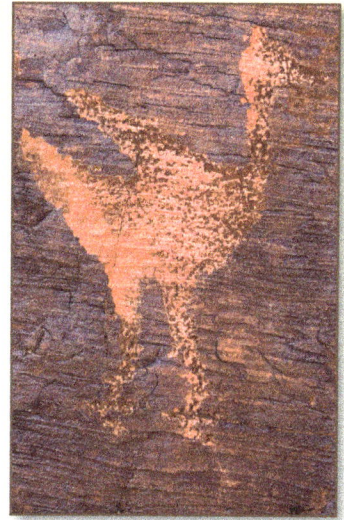

Birds

CHAPTER 10

Symbols in the Mountainair area which resemble birds may be associated with the bird katchinas such as the eagle, hawk, and turkey. In the winter solstice ceremony of the Hopi a number of birds are represented: the eagle, turkey, hummingbird, snipe, duck, owls, and two different hawks (Fewkes 1903:25). The bird symbols in the area may also be associated with some of the various bird clans that existed. For instance, the shield figure in Petroglyph 1 (Chapter 2, large panel, page 12) which is also pictured in a close-up in Chapter 11 (upper right, page 85) shows the hooked beak of an eagle and may denote the Eagle Clan. The head in Petroglyph 9 (Chapter 4, Section of agricultural panel, page 26) with a straighter beak and a turkey feather on its head possibly indicates a member of the Turkey Clan. The symbol in Petroglyph 27 resembles a hummingbird (also see Chapter 13, Figure 7, Agricultural panel, page 101). Duck, who was important in Pueblo mythology is shown in Petroglyph 28.

The figure in Petroglyph 27 is a combination of a hummingbird and person, or perhaps the Hummingbird Katchina. The symbol has both human and bird aspects. Features resembling a bird are the two small appendages, perhaps wings, or a tail, on the back. The face has a long, slightly curved line, a bill or beak, which is touching the flower, or bud, on the plant in front of it. Two long appendages also curve upward from the top of the head. Hummingbirds

PETROGLYPH 27 - Hummingbird with plant

have both straight and curved bills, short tails and several varieties have feather tufts and long crests curving backward from their heads (Miller et al 1987).

Human aspects of the figure are the hair, the body (possibly wearing a kilt), legs and feet, and one arm that is touching the stalk of the plant in front of it.

One very old, delicate Hopi Hummingbird Katchina has the long bill, a kilt or breechcloth, and what appears to be feathers attached to its head (Wright 1979:119). Considering the age of this katchina it would be closer to the actual, or realistic form than the modern ones that are being produced for the tourist trade.

Some animals and birds were thought to own, or possess certain plants or medicines. This was also true of the hummingbird. The Zuni called the Indian Paint Brush "hummingbird all sucking-food" because its blossoms are favored by that bird (Stevenson 1915:38,80). One clear way to show you own an item, or that it belongs to you, is to touch or hold it. The figure in Petroglyph 27 is touching the plant in front of it and may be indicating ownership or claiming that plant or medicine.

The structure of the plant shown with the hummingbird does not resemble Indian paintbrush but the single stem with off-set round fruit or berries can be seen in plants such as Manzanita, Common

Chokecherry, and Hawthorn (Elmore 1976: 124,142,146,147). All three plants are present in the Mountainair area. The leaves, bark, flowers, and haws of the Hawthorn (Viburnum) were all utilized by the American Indians for a number of medical treatments including: dysentery, stomach problems, cramps, colic, as a diuretic, for bladder problems, women's ailments, as a heart tonic, and as an application to swelling (Vogel 1970: 314-315).

Duck, Turkey, Sandhill Crane

Three birds, besides the eagle discussed in Chapter 7, that appear in the region and were important to the southwestern Indians were the duck, turkey, and sandhill crane. Birds were believed to carry messages from the deities and the duck plays an important part in Pueblo folklore.

Turkeys were held in captivity by the southwestern Indians for their feathers. Turkey feathers were used by the katchinas (Bunzel). Tradition placed them as the first feather on the Zuni prayersticks for Kokko (katchina), and the ancestors (Bol 1998:125). Turkey feathers, along with those of the duck, were also used on Keres prayersticks (Curtis 1970 VOL. XVI: 184) and wands placed on altars (Parsons 1966:688). One of the clans at Hopi was the Turkey Clan (Hodge 1912: 729).

Petroglyphs of the sandhill crane are often located on panels which also depict corn. There can be little doubt the birds shown are meant to represent the crane which is identified by its round head, long pointed beak, long neck and long legs with round knobby knees, see Petroglyph 14 (Chapter 5, Cornstalk, cranes and flute player, page 42). Crane Clans existed at Zuni, Tewa, and Hano (Hodge 1912:647, 657).

Duck

To the Zuni the duck, Petroglyph 28, "is not only a messenger, but the epiphany of a god" (Tyler 1964: 177) and the "most knowing of all creatures" (Dutton 1963:65).

Duck - PETROGLYPH 28

The Zuni believed their ancestors took the form of a duck to swim back up the Zuni River when their katchina dances were held (Bol 1998: 120-121), and in their mythology Duck plays a major role in the story of Kaklo, one of the rulers of the katchinas (Bunzel 1973:984-985). In the myth, Duck offers to guide Kaklo but he was unable to follow Duck into a lake that blocked the path. Rainbow-worm bent down to receive a prayerstick from Kakalo that bore duck feathers, and by bending and straightening, carried Kaklo to the shore of the sacred lake. In the end Kaklo was made keeper of the myths. Pictograph 10 (Chapter 4, Rainbow worm and bird, page 34) shows a rainbow with a duck-shaped figure standing on it, and on its back, a smaller bird/duck. Both figures face to the right. This panel may represent Rainbow-worm bearing Kaklo (the larger symbol) with its prayerstick offering of duck feathers symbolized by the smaller bird figure. The Kaklo Katchina carries a duck in one hand and around the face is painted the rainbow (ibid:980; Plate 28). The Hopi Duck Katchina also has a rainbow on both cheeks and "the scoop-shaped bill of a regular duck" (Wright 1979:112). The rainbow also transported Sia War Gods and Tewa Cloud Youths when they went courting (Parsons 1966:201) and the Zuni rainbow transported the Cloud People to earth (ibid:480).

Zuni tradition always places the duck feather second in order (after the eagle feather) on the prayersticks, which may also be a crook, of the Katchinas and the Ancestors, and third on the prayerstick of the Sun and of the Moon. The prayersticks, or pahos, were placed in cornfields to honor the spirits and ancestors (Bol 1998:125,127) and ones with cattails attached, brought by the Duck Kachina, were kept in houses (Wright 1979:112).

Duck feathers are used to sprinkle water (asperse) at Isleta, representing rainfall. This sprinkling of water is done among many pueblos, sometimes on canes of office, on corpses, in all the directions to bring the rain clouds, and on katchina dancers. When done on dancers it represents the rain falling on them to make them "strong and lively" (Parsons 1966:373-374). When duck feathers were placed in a bowl of water at Isleta by the War Chief it was said "the sounds of ducks playing and flapping their wings are heard" (ibid:728).

Turkey

The turkey in Petroglyph 11 (Chapter 4, Small panel with katchina and turkey, page 32), top center, depicts the bird standing on the ground with its large body, long tail, large wing, and short beak.

"Turkeys were raised in large numbers by all the Pueblo Indians from prehistoric times, as witness the numerous references to them by the earliest Spanish explores of the Southwest. Great numbers of turkey remains have been found in ruins of prehistoric pueblos as well as the pens in which they were confined" (Hodge, et al 1945:238). The Spanish explorer, Espejo, and his men were presented turkeys when they stopped at the Sia pueblo in 1582 (Parsons 1966:903).

Among the Pueblo Indians a single turkey feather may be worn at the crown of a persons head, or the entire tail attached around the waist (Parsons 1966: 645,647). The Mountainair Petroglyph 9 (Chapter 4, Section of agricultural panel, page 26) shows a figure that has a turkey shaped feather at the crown of the head. At Cochit, during the night of the dead, bundles of turkey feathers are buried at various locations and the dead are supposed to "decorate their heads with the feathers" (ibid: 858). At Taos the feathers are placed in specific locations for the dead and also offered at the sacred Blue Lake. "To Lightning, Cloud spirits, or kachina, tied turkey feathers are offered, in springs, in rivers, in lake, on the mountain" (Parsons 1966:290-291) and are also are associated with the rain cult (ibid: 275).

Excavations at Mound 7 at Grand Quivera produced turkey egg shell in nine rooms, one partial turkey skeleton, and two flutes made from the long bones of turkeys. Also, room number 108 was possibly used as a turkey pen (Hayes et al 1981: 46, 58, 150).

Hence, the turkey has been kept in captivity in the Southwest since prehistoric times, its feathers being used on prayersticks and by katchinas and its long bones used to make flutes. The turkey in the small panel of Petroglyph 11 (Chapter 4, page 32) is facing a figure with a horn curving from the middle of its head which perhaps represents male lightning and power for war.

Sandhill Crane

Petroglyph 29 (close-up of 14, Chapter 5, Cornstalk, cranes and flute player, page 42) shows the combined figure of a sandhill crane and flute player. The excavation at Mound 7 at Grand Quivera produced long bones (ulnae) from the sandhill crane and also three flutes made from their long bones (Hayes et al 1981: 206).

The following connects the crane and corn plant: Since the flute was played for the production of rain for the crops, including corn (Chapter 6), and flutes were made from bones of the crane, it's possible the sandhill crane was believed to bring moisture for the corn. In Petroglyph 14 we see the zigzag symbol of the snake/lightning

PETROGLYPH 29 - Fluteplayer and crane

touching one leg of the crane. This may indicate a flute made from the leg bone to attract lightning and rain. Notice the cornstalk on this panel has ears of corn and tassels showing successful growth from moisture.

A closer look at the symbol in Petroglyph 29 may further validate the connection between the crane and flute. This petroglyph contains elements of both a human and a crane. The figure stands upright and plays a flute, as only humans do. However, the elbows and knees are round, or knobby, resembling legs of the crane, and the lower body is bird-shaped with a short tail. The erect penis, representing virility or productivity, can be associated with the figures backpack. Transporting food or seeds can be done in a backpack or basket carried on the back, especially true among the American Indian. Thus, this figure, with elements of the crane (a water bird) is playing the flute to bring moisture for food production (productivity), which is indicated by a burden on its back. This figure associates the elements of the flute, the crane, food and humans and may represent the Crane Clan that existed among some of the Pueblo Indians.

At Zuni, the women of the Sandhill Crane Clan removed the seeds from the pods of a plant belonging to the Mustard family, named Ha'ko'lokta meaning 'sandhill crane' because this bird favored it. The seeds were crushed and mixed with the bean crop when it was planted thus causing the plants to become abundant. "This medicine belongs to the Sandhill Crane clan" (Stevenson 1915:85,91).

The sandhill cranes still visit the Mountainair area today. There are a number of watering tanks for the cattle located at windmills on the Chilton ranch that are kept stocked with goldfish to help keep the tanks clean. Periodically the Chiltons would observe a crane or other large water bird flying low over their property and they would subsequently find the goldfish were gone from the tanks and they would need to be restocked (personal communication 1982). In the fall of 2005 when photographs were being taken in the Mountainair region groups of sandhill cranes were observed headed south, presumably to the Bosque del Apache Reserve wintering grounds (author).

Thus, we see that duck, turkey and sandhill crane, all depicted in the Mountainair area, were important to those residents. Birds were important as messengers from the gods with the duck playing an important role in Zuni mythology. Its feathers, along with those of the turkey, were used on prayersticks. The turkey was kept in captivity in the Southwest from prehistoric times for its feather and flutes were made from the leg bones. Flutes were also made from the leg bones of the sandhill crane, and since flutes were used in the rainmaking ceremonies, the crane may be associated with the production of rain for the corn. We saw in Chapter 5 that corn was of the up most importance to the Pueblo Indians.

CHAPTER 11

Shields and Weapons

A variety of the large body shields are found in the Mountainair area along with two miniature ones in Petroglyph 10 (Chapter 4, Horned warriors and small shields, page 29). Shields are used for protection or to defend ones self and are associated with warfare so they sometimes appear with weapons such as spears. Shield figures are both pictographs and petroglyphs and fairly simple with some consisting of only a circle with a head shown above it. Others show only legs and a spear and one shield appears to have two people behind it showing two heads, four legs and a long spear or lance.

The large panel of Petroglyph 1 (Chapter 2, page 12) records the history of the village of Tinabo which is located on the above mesa. A close up of the shield figure of the Eagle Clan from that panel is shown at the top right on this page. This figure has the hooked beak of an eagle, legs and feet of a human, and is holding a spear showing the Eagle Clan as defending its village (Martineau, personal communication 1995).

Petroglyph 1 contains other symbols of warfare: an arrowshaft with fletching or feathers, a spear point, and a reflex bow. The snake directly to the left of the Eagle Shield figure means to strike and the bare feet on the panel mean exposed or danger. The inverted human figure on the far right means dead (Martineau 1973, pg160). The bow to the right of the Eagle Shield symbol has a lions' leg and foot with exposed claws. Felines bare their claws to fight or attack. The large lion to the far right on the panel appears to have its claws knocked off or damaged and may indicate the Lion Clan was declawed or defeated. A close up of this lion is at the top right on page 51, Chapter 7. Thus, Petroglyph 1 shows Tinabo belonged to the Eagle Clan and there was danger and warfare and people died. The lion symbols indicate the village was attacked by the Lion Clan. The University of Calgary conducted a field school at Tinabo in 1981 and 1982 and recovered a beam from the kiva. The last tree ring to grow on the beam was added in A.D. 1466 telling us it was cut at that date to use in construction (Baldwin 1988) so this was the time period in which the village was being built.

One beautifully painted circular shield has only a dish-shaped head associated with it (back cover). However, not all shields are circular. A rectangular shield and head are shown in Pictograph 14 which is very faded. The shield is outlined in red, the face (or mask) in black with white and turquoise objects on top. This figure very possibly represents a katchina.

The largest shield figure observed is approximately three feet long, see Petroglyph 2 (Chapter 2, Large star shield figure, page 13); Figure 6 (Chapter 9, Large star shield figure, page 75). This is one of two I have located in the area with a star. It has legs with feet

PICTOGRAPH 14 - Rectangular shield and mask

and toes, a round head and mouth, round eyes, and nine triangles radiating out from the head. These triangles may represent the sun or arrowheads (Martineau 1973, 160). The other smaller star shield figure shows the profile of a running person that has realistically human shaped legs and a face that appears to have a long bird or duck beak.

One upright figure, Petroglyph 30, resembles a turtle from the shape of its head and beak and short pointed tail. Again the legs and feet are human shaped so this may represent the Turtle Clan. It is an interesting symbol as shields are protective and the shell of a turtle is also hard and protective. During dances members of the Hopi Snake Society and Men's Society wear a turtle shell rattle on their right knee and the rattling sound is said to attract the thunder. Turtles used in ceremonies were collected from different areas with permission first granted from the spirits (Parsons 1966: 384-5).

A group of three shield figures, Petroglyph 31, is very unusual. The top figure appears damaged and is somewhat hard to make out but the spiral one on the left can be clearly seen and ends at the top with what apparently is a head. The third figure, lower right, appears to have human legs with bent knees and a long neck and a head. In this shield is a dragonfly symbol indicated by the double set of wings and attached to the back of the shield is a tiny set of wings and may indicate flying. This panel also contains bird symbols.

Another spiral symbol may be seen in Petroglyph 32. It has human legs bent at the knees and a head that resembles a crane with an open beak that can indicate calling or asking for a favor. The figure is standing on the head of a person holding a bow in its right hand and a possible war club or ceremonial object of an animal in its left. Many ceremonial items and bags were made of animal pelts and the object in the left hand has four straight vertical lines on the bottom that may represent legs. Early Plains Indians are pictured dancing with bows and arrows, spears, shields, and smaller carved items to which feathers, hair, deer dew claws, and other objects are attached (Lowie 1982: figures 32, 64, 66, 69 and 79). One Plains Indian ceremonial carving shows a staff with a crane's head and an open mouth, or bill (ibid: figure 80)

Turtle shield - PETROGLYPH 30

that closely resembles the head and mouth at the top of the spiral shield in this petroglyph.

Some insight may be gained into the figures in Petroglyphs 31 and 32 by examining the Zuni Shumakwe Society which was named after the dragonfly (Dutton 1963:83-85). The society was named after "a spiral shell, because the fraternity treats for convulsions-terrible twisting of the body... (and) The Shumaikoli of the six regions are patrons of the fraternity, together with their warriors, Saiapa" (ibid:84). The warriors mentioned are the Beast Gods discussed in Chapter 7. The petroglyphs both contain a spiral "shield" and the one in Petroglyph 32 is standing on the head of a warrior, although not one of the Beast Gods. However, in Petroglyph 31, the bird at the far right has the shape of an eagle which is a Beast God. Officers for the Shumaikoli Society could have been from only three specific clans, one of which was the Sandhill Crane Clan and the figure directly to the left of the dragonfly shield resembles a crane. "The dragon fly doubtless symbolizes the carrying of a message for aid to the supernatural ones and the Shumaikoli priests" (Dutton 1963:85). Thus, in the latter two petroglyphs we have the dragonfly, messenger to the Gods; the spiral or twisting shape (convulsions); the sandhill crane with its mouth open (possibly appealing to the Gods); and a hunter or warrior with a bow. All of these symbols are related to the

PETROGLYPH 31 - Shield figures

Spiral shield standing on warrior - PETROGLYPH 32

Shumakwe Society at Zuni. Other symbols in the area show figures holding weapons and wearing headdresses. Pictograph 4 (Chapter 3, Hunter with bow, page 18), shows a man with a bow in his right hand and a head ornament and is directly overhead and above the yellow mountain lion in Chapter 2 (Pictograph 1, page 14).

"Clubs and battle-axes are extremely effective—and significant—early weapons of war" (LeBlanc 1999; 95) and are visible on panels. These would have been used in close, hand to hand combat. The Eagle Shield figure, upper right, page 85, holds a longer spear, or lance in association with a shield. Shields constructed of wicker were made in the southwest by the mid to late 1200s, followed by hide shields when the more powerful recurved bow replaced the self-bow (ibid: 97-98).

The prehistoric self-bows are long and straight before being strung and are reportedly fairly weak. The unstrung recurved bow is shaped like what we today call a cupid's bow and may be constructed of wood, elk, or mountain sheep horn (author). These are backed with layer of deer sinew (tendon) which is applied with glue that may be made from boiled hoof. The more layers of sinew added, the more powerful the bow. Having witnessed both prehistoric models of the self-bow and recurved bow shot, the recurved is much more powerful. There are early records of arrows shot from recurved bows that penetrated the chain mail (armor made of metal plates) worn by Spanish explorers. The self-bow in the Southwest dates from circa A.D. 200 and the recurved bow between A.D. 1100 and the mid 1400s (LeBlanc 1999; 101). Petroglyphs and pictographs displaying the recurved bow verify that symbols of these on panels were made in the time period of A.D. 1100 to the mid 1400s or later. Recurved bow symbols from murals at Hopi and Pottery Mound have helped assign dates of the 1400s (ibid: 102).

In conclusion, a number of different types of shields appear in the Mountainair area. They are of various sizes and range from very basic to more detailed ones. Some appear to represent birds and one a turtle. These may be associated with warfare and also ceremonies and dances, as with the Plains Indians. Figures holding bows, spears, or staffs and other possible ceremonial objects are also present. Depictions of the recurved bow help to date panels they appear on since that type of bow replaced the self-bow in the southwest circa AD 1100 to the mid 1400s.

CHAPTER 12

Miscellaneous

Hand and Foot Prints

Numerous types of footprint symbols are found in the Mountainair region. Various types, both human and animal, are seen on the large panel in Petroglyph 1 (Chapter 2, page 12). On the far left is a pair of human prints. In the center of the panel, above the natural crack in the sandstone, is a leg with five long, curved claws that appear to be lion. This type of claw also appears on the large animal to the right. In the center of the panel (below the crack) is a set of cloven hooves, possibly bison. Below this symbol is the square print with five long curved claws and a circle where each claw is attached to the foot. Birds tracks are also present on some petroglyphs panels.

In most cases human footprints appear very realistic and are found on both horizontal and vertical surfaces. Pairs of them are found side by side and other times they are off-set to make it appear they are walking across the surface of the rock. In a couple areas the footprints "walk" to the edge of a horizontal surface and stop. This gives the impression the feet walked to the edge of the rock and disappeared over the side.

Many deer tracks are found in the area consisting of pairs either with or without the dew claws present. The concept of "fleeing" or running comes from the fact that the dew claws on a deer never make an imprint except when the deer is running (Martineau 1973: 142-143). Thus, deer tracks with the dew claws represent scared or danger as a deer will run when it feels threatened or is spooked. Petroglyph 33 is an exception as it shows the whole leg of the deer with the hoof and dew claws. The Aztec were "more artistic in their depictions, and meticulously show the entire hoof and dew claws in profile" (ibid:142-143). Although this leg is not in profile, it is the only deer leg of this type located in the area.

As mentioned above, Petroglyph 1 shows what appears to be the leg of a mountain lion with very long, curved extended claws. Matsaki Polychrome bowls, which were not produced after 1680, were found during the excavation of the Zuni site at Hawikuh, and are painted with the same design of a leg and extended curving claws (Smith et al. 1966:332,: Fig. 53a and Fig. 60g). In Chapter 7 we saw that the mountain lion was one of the Zuni Beast Gods.

The largest percentage of human handprints are realistically portrayed. These can be seen on the large panel in Petroglyph 1 (Chapter 2, page 12) left of center, and in Petroglyph 3 (Chapter 2, page 16) where they are associated with lightly pecked facial features.

Stepped Elements

The stepped elements, mentioned in Chapter 4, are associated with a number of different symbols. These steps denote terraced, piled up, mountain (Martineau 1974:138-139, symbol 17). The stepped design forms the headdress of the Hopi Corn Maid (Shalako Mana) which also contains the chin stripe, corn symbol, clouds, lightning and rain (Fewkes 1973:175). On this design the top step symbol is elevated to the level with the lightning and rain clouds. This symbol is also on the Sumaikoli Shields which, like the Corn Maid, are associated with rain, vegetation and corn, thus productivity (Stephen 1936: 821-822). This design is also present on tiles of the Flute Altar Society where the flute is being played for a corn plant located on the top of a mound which sets atop a stepped symbol (ibid: Plate XXII). Faces/masks both humans and birds also have this stepped element incorporated into them.

The stepped design can be seen in architecture at a Taos, New Mexico, church with crosses

PETROGLYPH 33
Deer leg with dew claws

located on top. This design with a cross on top is present at one of the Mountainair petroglyphs and may relate to the Spanish built missions and is located near a symbol which appears to be a padre with a broad brimmed hat riding a mule.

In many cases the design appears to be associated with productivity as it is associated with being elevated and in the heavens with other symbols such as clouds, lightning, and rain. The symbol with a cross on its top would relate to the heavens also as it is elevating people, or their prayers, up to a higher position and the gods.

Heart lines on animals

The Zuni Indians painted figures on their vessels showing a "heart line." The heart line "from the mouth to the animal's interior is distinctively Zuni" and was painted on ceramics (Sturtevant 1979:477). Petroglyphs 12 (Chapter 4, Lion with headdress and heartline, page 38), and 34 both show animals with a heart line to their interior. Petroglyph 12 is a "long tail" or mountain lion while the large figure in Petroglyph 34 resembles a bear. The latter has both the heart line and also an arrow in the posterior of its body. Some prehistoric hunters believed that drawing an animal with the heart line would make their arrow go straight to the animals heart and bring a successful hunt.

Maiden hair-whorls

Petroglyph 35 shows an example in the Mountainair region that portrays the hair-whorls of a Hopi maiden. Young Hopi girls let their hair grow and fashioned it on the sides of their heads in this style until married. After the maidens are married their hair is cut at the base of their neck. These hair-whorls can still be seen on the unmarried females among the Hopi today and appears on the Hopi Katchina Maiden, the Heheya Kachina-mana, and the Hemis Katchina Maiden (Colton 1959: 29, 51 and fig. 11).

Stone Features and Small Shelters

Mention should be made of man-made monuments such as rock piles, both small and large, stone circles and boundary markers. Many people are unaware Native Americans constructed and utilized such spots. Large rock shelters or overhangs are very obvious and many times used by early people for reasons such as shelter, storing items, or burials. Very small or tiny shelters, like the ones I discovered with pictographs in them, are easy to bypass due to their size and initially appeared too small for a person to have worked in.

It is possible for man-made features to blend in so well with the landscape they go unnoticed. Once your eyes are trained to observe these places along trails, springs, and near village sites their presence becomes quiet evident. The boundary marker, shrine, or stone post, being ambiguous have "attracted little attention from students of the Pueblo… (and) any information is valuable" (Tyler 1964:26). I believe these features are of value no matter where their location.

Some Southwestern groups still recognize stone monuments today and place offerings at them. This was observed on the road leading up to third mesa, Polacca, Arizona, on the Hopi reservation. Non-Hopis may not enter this area without a Hopi Indian to accompany them. One of the reasons given was that people would stop and take items from shrines like the one we passed on the road (author). The Hopi also used specific symbols placed on rocks to mark limits or boundaries of land holdings (Titiev 1992:62).

A large rock pile, three feet high, is located in the Lava Beds National Monument in northern California, once home of the Modoc Indians. It is situated several feet off a trail that connects some of the lava tubes. A NPS employee stated that when the Modoc

PETROGLYPH 34 - Large animal with heart line

inhabited this area travelers passing the rock pile would place a stone on it asking for a safe journey (author).

In central Arizona's Tonto Basin, there are small piles of stones, not native to that area, near the perimeter of prehistoric village sites. One distinct trail follows a ridge, leading south out of the Tonto Basin, toward the direction of present day Phoenix. It passes a small rock circle, which from considering erosion, appeared to have been in that spot for a number of years. The trail then passes through a prehistoric village site located in the saddle of a ridge with boulders at either end containing petroglyph symbols. When showing the boulder on the upper end of the village site to LaVan Martineau in 1992 he studied the petroglyphs and then said it was a "spirit rock." On the uphill side of this large rock was a small hole in the ground that seemed deep and even on this warm day contained cool air. Mr. Martineau said spirits often protected villages and the guardian for this village lived in the hole beneath this boulder.

This Tonto Basin trail, after passing through the village, then proceeds on south, passing several large stone circles, or enclosures. The stone circles along this path no doubt had a special significance to the prehistoric people who once used it. Cattle use this trail today and it could be attributed to them if the prehistoric features were not present. No doubt many stone monuments have been destroyed over the years by agriculture, homesteading, ranching and other activities. The ones mentioned above are in a fairly isolated area and so far unaffected by present day activity.

Prayersticks and other offering were, and are still, placed at certain spots for various reasons. When visiting Mesa Verde in 1985 prayersticks had been placed by one of the Native American groups at a spring located against the back wall in a ruin our guide took us through.

In the Mountainair area, three very tiny rock shelters were discovered which contained pictographs. All three shelters were so small it was only possible to see into them by lying with your back and head on the ground. One contained a face with eyes, a mouth, and appeared to be wearing a hat. The painting had somewhat deteriorated and had been applied in yellow, white, black, and red. Since the shelters had been visited in prehistoric time and had figures painted in them it is possible they were used for shrines in which

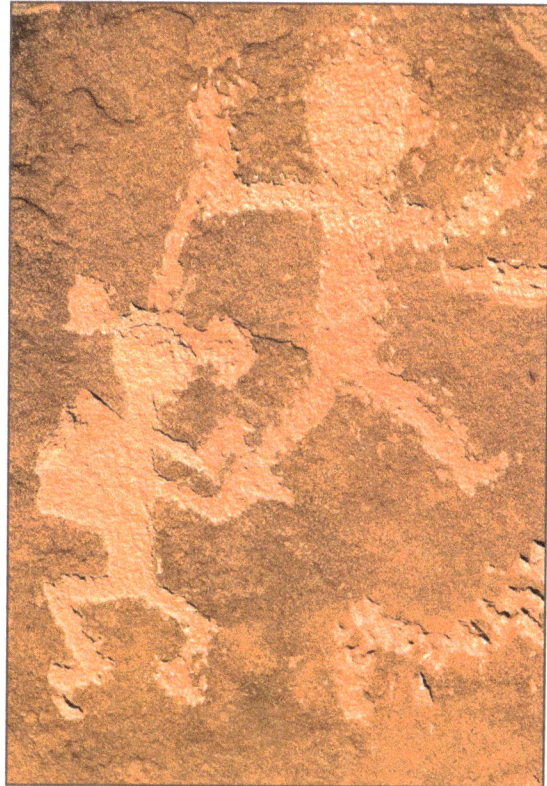

PETROGLYPH 35
Hopi maiden with hair whorls

offerings were placed. Shrines are found in caves, on ledges, near springs, in fields, and on hill tops in the forms of stone circles, rock piles, pit shrines or elaborate altars and, due to their powerful nature, were considered dangerous areas (Parsons 1966:307-311).

A number of circles are located on the panel examined in Chapter 13 (Figure 7, pages 100-101) which I believe records agriculture. Parts of the panel are shown in Petroglyphs 9 (Chapter 4, Section of agricultural panel, page 26); 27 (Chapter 10, Hummingbird with plant, page 78) and 36. The panel contains a Shalako figure which brings the rain and also a symbol which appears to represent nectar or pollen collecting. Stones were placed in the field as fertility markers and perhaps the circles on the panel represent the type of marker that would be associated with rain and the growth, or plant production. This concept may appear ambiguous but the use of stone boundary markers has been found in the Southwestern United States placed in corners to mark territory. The Zuni Indians used stones to mark the borders of their fields. Before leaving the safety of their mesa, the Hopi visited a rock shrine to Masu'u, their deity of travelers, who is also a powerful god of boundaries (Tyler 1964:25-26).

PETROGLYPH 36 - Coiled snake on agricultural panel

The above use of stone boundary markers by prehistoric people may sound very unlikely to us today but consider how we mark our boundaries. We post signs with such messages as "DO NOT ENTER, KEEP OUT PRIVATE PROPERTY." We have roadside monuments along traveled routes at which people may stop. We also construct monuments in the form of buildings, landmarks, cemeteries, and altars in churches at which we leave offerings in the form of flowers, crosses and other objects.

After considering the information on prehistoric peoples, their belief system, and their gods it is only logical to conclude they also placed markers or signs to communicate to others, to mark their territory, or as a location to leave offerings.

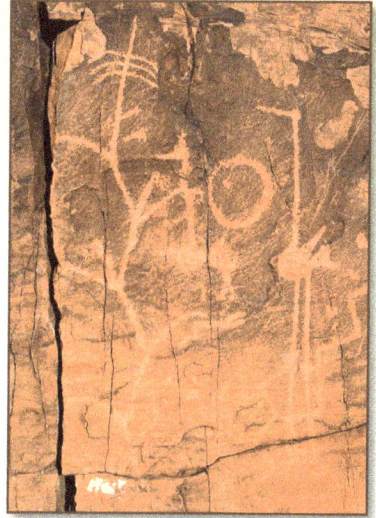

CHAPTER 13

Agricultural Panel

The panel in Figure 7, is partly shown in Petroglyphs 9 (Chapter 4, page 26); 27 (Chapter 10, page 78); and 36 (Chapter 12, page 96) and unique enough to be discussed separately. Due to the very difficult nature to photograph it the sketch in Figure 7 was completed to show all the symbols present. This panel has been left until last because a number of previous chapters contain an explanation of some of its symbols that are associated with crops, moisture and agriculture. Its location is different than the others which are located on outcrops, ridges, or in rock shelters and overhangs. This panel is located on a slanted slab of rock lying in the bottom of a wash where water would flow during flash flooding. Since the panel deals with moisture for crops the bottom of a wash is an appropriate location. A number of symbols are either partially of completely covered with pecking, which may indicate moisture or wet (Martineau 1973: 25; 63). This pecking is indicated by the dots present on the symbols in Figure 7. The panel also contains a number of cupules, explained below. Few cupules are found on panels in the Mountainair region. One small panel contains these deeply pecked circular depressions and a few other panels contain an isolated cupule or two associated with petroglyphs.

Among the symbols on this panel are: five squares (enclosures, boundaries, gardens); one Shalako; three long horn figures; one

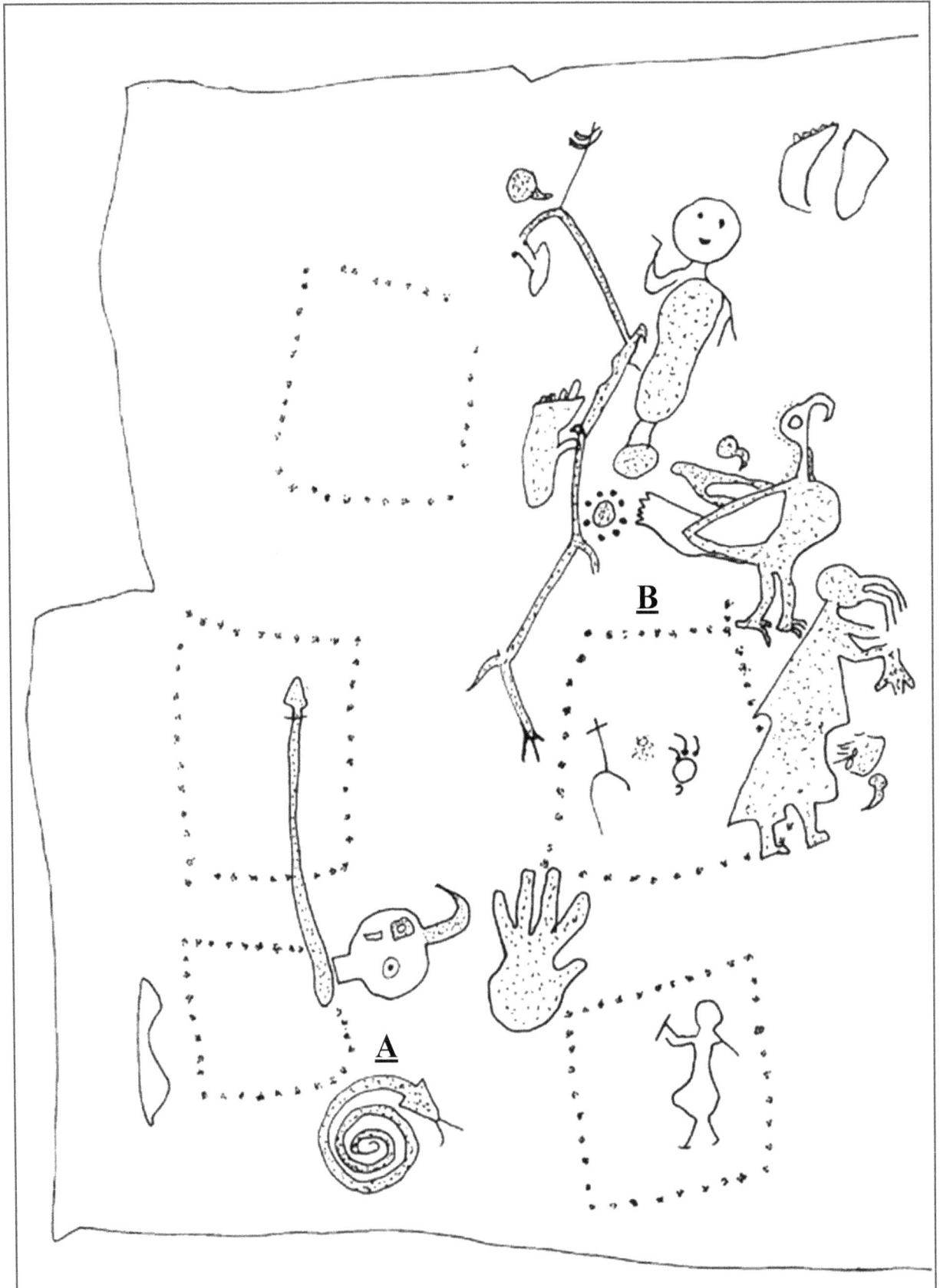

FIGURE 7 - Agricultural panel (left side)

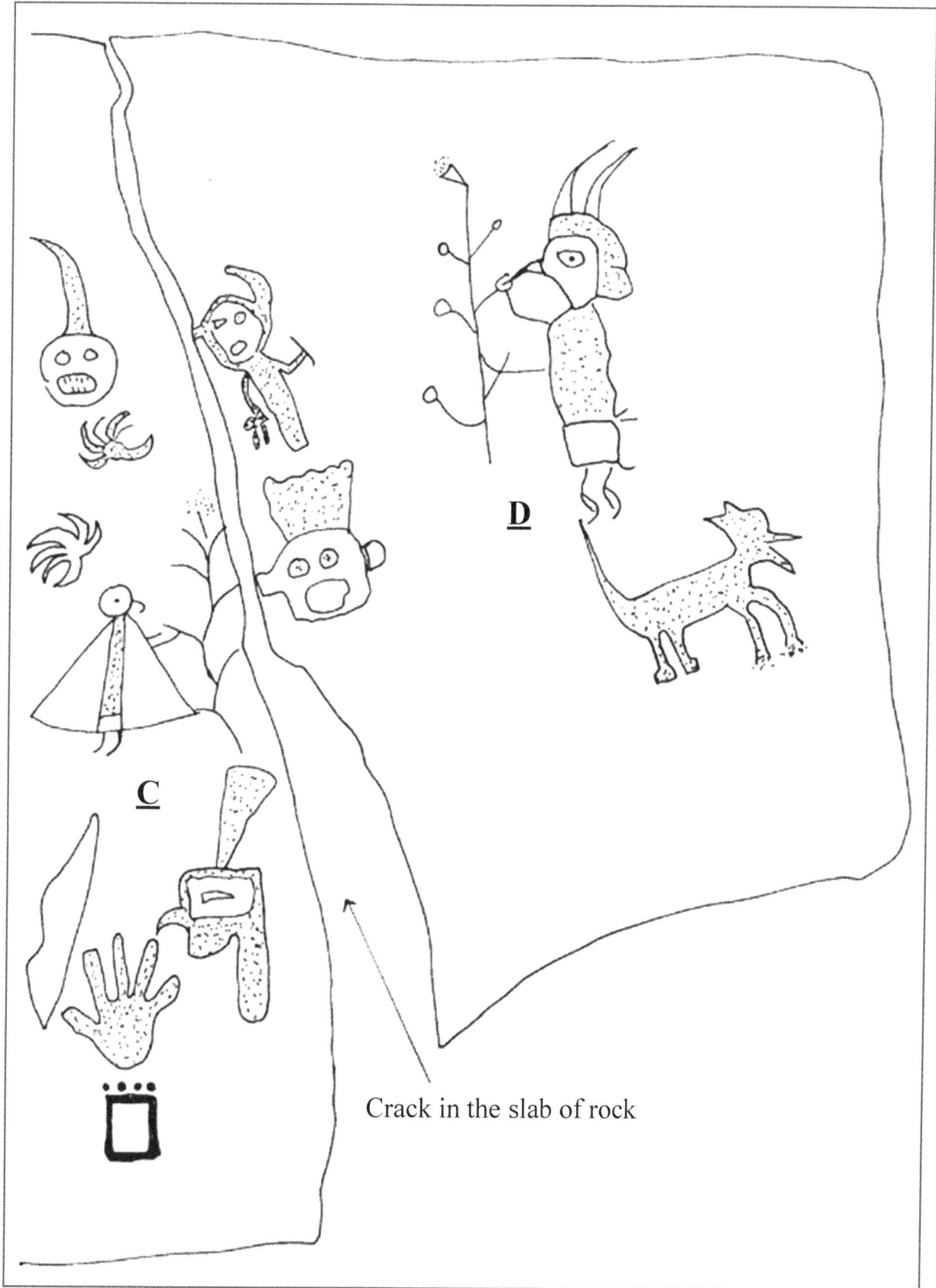

Crack in the slab of rock

(right side) Agricultural panel - FIGURE 7

definite corn stalk; three figures associated with, or touching, plants (one of which is possibly corn); one coiled snake; two bows (war chiefs or Shikames); hand and footprints; one turkey; one head with both turkey and human aspects, and one canine figure.

Enclosures or Gardens

Five square and/or rectangular shaped areas (garden spaces) whose outlines are made of cupules are present in areas marked **A** and **B**. Cupules are cup-shaped depression pecked to varying depths in rock. These may be on either flat, angular, or upright panels and their significance is undecided among anthropologist. Cupules located on angular or vertical panels would not actually hold water or moisture and may be symbolic of a depression in which water would be contained. If so, this would verify these are actually gardens or planting areas, where water is necessary for the growth of crops. The other deep cupule symbols in the area are on a small horizontal panel on a hillside, not close to a present day wash although a natural spring is located in the vicinity.

Garden spaces are located near ruins in the Mountainair area. These are visible today and consist of rock outlines protruding above the grounds surface forming either square or rectangular shapes. The outlines are on gentle slopes and may have been constructed to help retain moisture during rains. This would have been the only source of water available for crops other than sparsely scattered springs at varying distances from habitation sites. Garden spaces were mentioned in Chapter 6 on the flute player. They are found pictured on tiles from the Hopi Flute Society Altar (Stephen 1936:Plate XXII); were observed in the southwest in the 1880s (Bandelier 1975:407); and are found at Zuni where they were used to contain water for the plants within them (Bol 1998:120). The panel in Figure 7 is slanted to make the actual rock outlines lie on a gentle slopes, an example of rock incorporation. That along with the concave cupules give us two rock associations that may relate the symbols to actual garden plots on slopes and the retention of moisture. Four of the five enclosures contain symbols, the one at upper left being empty and located next to a corn stalk, to its right, which appears uprooted and dead. This may indicate a barren or dead field with nothing growing in it.

Shalako and Longhorns

The enclosure below the letter **B** shows a Shalako exiting its right side. Shalako dancers are very tall (10 to 12 feet), clothed in 2 garments, or capes and carry prayersticks or offerings in their hands. This figure fits that criteria. Parsons (1966:746-758) gives a good description of the annual ceremony which lasts almost the whole year during which the Shalako and Long Horns meet almost every night. The Shalako, present in many pueblo ceremonies, is associated with bringing crops, animals and prosperity to the people (Sturtevant 1979: 500) and they also bring warm days and sweep away the old year. The one on this panel carries an object in its right hand, possibly an offering or prayersticks. On the figures back, with one foot touching it, stands a turkey. The Pueblo Indians kept turkeys in captivity for years and raised them for their feathers which were used on prayersticks (Chapter 10).

The turkey has its head up and tilted back as if swallowing water. This is the way fowl drink water, they raise their head and tilt it backwards for water to run down their throat. Most of the turkey symbol and the whole Shalako figure has been pecked, again an indication of moisture, rain or being wet. This may indicate the Shalako ceremonies were successful in bringing prosperity in the form of rain to benefit the crops and animals, or it may just be verifying the purpose of the ceremony.

One ceremony photographed circa 1896 recorded six Shalako dancers which, after entering the village, planted prayersticks asking for the prosperity of the people, crops, and animals (Sturtevant 1979: 500). It was not mentioned if all Shalako were dressed in like manner or not. However, a modern Sio Shalako, combining both Hopi and Zuni elements of dress was first recorded in 1893. Four were present at the dance, two male and two female figures (Wright 1994: 142-143). (Sio is also found spelled Zia and Sia.)

The one horned god exists among the pueblo and for the Hopi guards the underworld and the two paths the departed souls will travel on (Colton 1959:79). The long horns work with the Shalako and the war priest and two of the three long horns on the panel have one round eye and one long (rectangular) eye. One is located just above the letter **A** and the other is the upper figure just right of the crack in the slab of rock. The one small eye is for the witch people, so they will have a short life; the one longer eye is for the good people, so they will live a long life (Parsons 1966:748). The third long horn, the upper figure located to the left of the crack, has one long pecked curved horn rising from the center of its head. This may represent lightning (Tyler 1964:100-101) and being pecked can indicate rain or moisture, which the lightning would bring. The longhorns also took part in telling when to plant corn, could also act as war chiefs and also told migration stories.

Below the Shalako is a third enclosure which contains one figure. The last two fields are located to the left and are connected by a long, curved symbol resembling a spear or arrow with an arrow head on its upper end. Directly to its right is one of the long horn figures.

Also associated with this square are a coiled snake and one of two bows on the panel.

Bows

Bows are normally assumed to be associated with warfare. However, this is not their only meaning. The Bow Priests are also referred to as a war chief and Shikame (Parsons 1966: Table1 Ceremonial Organization). I believe one meaning of the bows on this panel is the association with agriculture since the Bow Priest is in charge of the game and food supply, including the wild food. He is also in "charge of the communal cornfields, directing planting, tilling, and harvesting" and also rain-making (ibid: 132, 926, 884). The Bow Priest and Snake Societies are also curing societies with the snake a patron of the Corn Clan. The Shikame and Snake Societies are two that cure for witchcraft (Parsons 1966:132, 893, 900) and may explain why the symbols of the snake and bow are on this panel along with enclosures (or fields), plants and longhorns whose eyes are associated with life spans of good and evil people.

Both bows on this panel are recurved bows which replaced the straight, or self-bow and made their appearance between A.D. 1100 and the mid-1400s. This would indicate these symbols were made in that time period or later.

Corn

Two plants which represent corn stalks appear on this panel. The one above the letter **C** is in contact with an insect, possibly a butterfly. Insects similar to this one with wings, legs and curved projections extending from their mouths were found painted on both Matsaki and Hawikuh Polychrome vessels excavated at Zuni (Smith et al 1966: Fig. 72, Fig. 77) and date in the 1400s. The structure of this symbol does indicate a corn plant and the pecking at its top may indicate pollen, gathered by the Pueblo Indians and used in many ceremonies to represent "growth or new life" (Parsons1966; 481). If the insect is a butterfly it would tie in with corn as different colored butterflies are associated with the various colored corn, bring rain, and butterfly symbols are found painted on katchina helmets, a type of mask (ibid: 172, 773).

The larger of the two plants, to the left of **B**, appears to be dead. Its roots are showing, which indicates it is not planted, or in the ground, and it has no ears of corn. This symbol also appears on Hawikuh Polychrome vessels (ibid: Fig.74 f; Fig.76 b). Two symbols are connected to the stalk, a footprint on the left and a human figure on the right. A bare footprint means unprotected or exposed to danger (Martineau 1973:103) therefore the one attached to the cornstalk could mean the corn was in danger and was killed or died. The figure to the right of the corn is connected by a line touching the area where a person's stomach would be located. If there is no food (corn) to eat, for your stomach, you go hungry. Above the line connecting the corn to the stomach, the figure is indented, or being "cut in two" from hunger (ibid: 74, 75). This may indicate why the enclosure to the left is empty, the fields themselves were barren and people went hungry even though these symbols are also pecked or "wet." Major droughts were experienced in the southwest approximately every two hundred years leading to the starvation of populations and abandonment of areas. One such dry spell, recorded by the Spanish, occurred in the mid 1600s with the previous drought in the 1400s.

To the right of the two cornstalks is a third plant, above the letter **D**, and is associated with what resembles a hummingbird, Petroglyph 27, (Chapter 10, page 78) and below the hummingbird, a coyote (Chapter 7). The plant the hummingbird is touching has a stalk with off-set single branches and one round object on the end of each. The structure of this plant suggests Viburnum, also known as low bush cranberry, nannyberry or black haw. This plant grows in the southwest and after the flowers appear in May, a red to blackish fruit appears. This fruit, or haws, will remain into winter unless it is eaten by "numerous small birds or animals" (Elmore 1976: 146). All parts of the plant (bark, root, fruit, leaves, flowers) were utilized as medicine by the American Indians for dysentery, cramps, colic, a diuretic tea, bladder ailments, women's medicine, for an application to swellings, and stomach ailments (Vogel 1970: 314, 315). Claims are made that the "roots can cure diabetes and even varicose veins" (Elmore 1976:146). If the fruit is red, we know hummingbirds are attracted to red, and by touching the plant, the Hummingbird Clan may be claiming this plant, or medicine.

Directly below the hummingbird is located a pecked coyote/wolf figure. This may represent "water coyote" (Parsons 1966: 285). The mouth of the coyote is open, as if calling or talking. As discussed in Chapter 7, the Navajo and Pueblo Indians both possessed this canine figure. Among the Navajo the coyote calls the rain, and killing the coyote results in no rain or moisture. (Luckert 1979: 228). Coyote may also be responsible for good health and general blessing (ibid: 9), although we did see earlier that coyote can also bring death. This opened mouth canine symbol may represent water coyote calling the rain for crop production.

The panel in Figure 7 contains a number of symbols which may be related to crop production and moisture. We have enclosures, boundary markers, or garden spaces; symbols which are responsible for bringing moisture like the Shalako, snake, the long horns, and water coyote. Also, pecking on a number of the symbols, indicating wet or moisture; and the location of the panel which is in the bottom of a canyon on the side of a wash. A relative date for this panel would be after A.D. 1100 since there are recurved bows present. Taking into account barren fields, the dead corn, and person cut in half from hunger the symbols may indicate the rain ceremonies were not productive and the drought of the mid 1400s was occurring.

Conclusions

The Mountainair, New Mexico, area shows evidence of intermittent human occupation dating from Paleo-Indian times (10,000 to 8,000 B.C) until its abandonment by the Pueblo Indians in the late 1600s, thus spanning approximately 11,000 years. The area includes the present day ruins of Abó, Gran Quivira and Quarai, the Salinas Pueblo Missions National Monument. The Pueblo Indians that inhabited the area in the late 1500s when the Spanish arrived were the ancestors of the ancient Anasazi who had lived in the four corners area. Two of their distinctive attributes were the kiva and above ground rectangular, masonry houses with contiguous rooms, some being multi-storied. Both of these features are present in the Mountainair region. Early written records from the Spanish stated the area had around 800 inhabitants at their time of arrival. Over the years those Indians were impacted by many forces—the Spanish who attempted to Christianize them and used them as slaves to construct their missions and to gather and transport salt from the Estancia Basin to Mexico; Apache raids which destroyed Abó Mission; and droughts and famines which occurred every two hundred years. The above disturbances, especially those by the Spanish, resulted in some of these Eastern Pueblo Indians to seek temporary refuge among the Western Pueblos for a period of time, placing them in contact with the Hopi and Zuñi. When the Mountainair area was finally abandoned in the late 1600s, many inhabitants relocated to the El Paso-Juarez area to the south.

The early residents of the Mountainair area left behind proof of their existence and beliefs in the form of petroglyphs and pictographs. Influences from the Hopi and Zuñi are evident in various symbols discussed. Dates for petroglyph and pictograph panels in the Mountainair region may vary widely due to the long period of occupation. Some petroglyphs appear very old exhibiting substantial amounts of desert varnish, or patina, that has collected over the years. However, patina is not a reliable dating method. Content of some panels may offer relative proof of their age. The Abó Painted Rocks Site, near Abó Mission, contains symbols comparable to Pottery Mound, near Albuquerque, and Kuaua, north of Albuquerque. The beginning date for all three is approximately A.D. 1300 with dates of abandonment ranging from A.D. 1450 to 1672. Some petroglyph and pictograph symbols are identical to those painted on vessels excavated at the Zuñi site of Hawikuh dating from A.D. 1475 to the mid 1600s. Symbols of recurved bows are found on panels; these weapons came into use in the southwest circa A.D. 1100 to the mid 1400s. Petroglyphs of people riding a mule or horse would date to Spanish contact or later due to the fact that these animals entered the southwest with the Spanish explorers in the late 1500s.

Some symbols resemble figures painted on historic pottery and ceremonial objects on altars that were observed and recorded by Southwestern anthropologist. This dates them to historic times and indicates they were used over a period of years, perhaps surviving from prehistory. More recent research suggests the possible origin of some ceremonies and symbols such as the katchinas and the Zuñi water serpent may have originated in Mesoamerica with similarities observed between the Aztec, Hopi, and Zuñi gods. Facial and body elements in the area have a strong resemblance to the Jornado Mogollon (originating in Mexico) with Mimbres, Anasazi, and Great Plains elements also present. Thus, as stated above, dates for panels and symbols may vary widely but some are able to be assigned approximate dates due to their content.

We are very fortunate that the inhabitants of the area placed their symbols upon the sandstone and that early ethnologist and anthropologist who worked and lived among the Pueblo Indians recorded their observations in detail. By studying these records we are able to find clues relating to ceremonies, belief systems and the way of life of these people and their struggle to survive overwhelming odds.

Some of the conclusions we may draw by comparing the panel content with documented records are as follows:

The people of the Mountainair area recognized at least four of the same Beast Gods, or Gods of the Prey, that the Zuñi did: the Mountain Lion, Coyote/Wolf, Eagle and Mole. The Mountain Lion, the most important Prey God is associated with hunting, certain curing rites and as a guardian. It is present in the form of stone effigies, a yellow pictograph (yellow often symbolizing north) and petroglyphs. One pair of lions located in Abó Pass, the entrance to the important salinas, or salt beds to the east and neighboring pueblos, may represent the Lion Clan standing guard at this spot.

Petroglyphs of the eagle are often located up high, or near the top of panels, thus representing it as God of the Upper Regions. One eagle painted in white may represent the eastern skies. Another eagle is painted in red with X's on its back representing the eagle's wings. The profile of an eagle's head located on another panel possibly denotes Bird God, who was always present in the spring equinox ceremony of the Hopi.

Coyote/Wolf, who is interchangeable, has a rich tradition in southern lore. He is depicted as water coyote (calling the rain) on an agricultural panel in the area and is accompanied with other plant and game symbols. Coyote taught the Zuñi how to hunt and at night he called sickness. Thus, Coyote was made to live in the hills as they did not want sickness and death close by.

Mole, guardian of the underworld, is found pecked in a well-hidden, recessed area. Mole represents the underground and concealment. Although small and less imposing as a Beast God, Mole also played a very important part in mythology and assisted the Hopi in the destruction of both Winged Snake and Bird Monster. It was also a spirit helper for young men during their initiation into Shaman Ceremonies. References to Mole are also present in the Aztec legends of South America. These Prey Gods played a very important part in the ceremonial life of the Western and Eastern Pueblo Indians.

The snake or serpent, often associated with lightning, water and the Rain Gods is well represented in the area and is also found farther south among the Aztec and Toltecs. Snakes were also important to the Hopi and Zuñi Indians. One pictograph portrays the Hopi water serpent, Palolokon, and also possibly Quetzacoatl, the horned and feathered serpent of Mesoamerica. Another snake, which appears to be rising from a circle with an eagle's head directly to its right, may represent the Hopi equinox ceremony performed yearly to draw the sun back across the sky for the continuation of life and for bringing new life and fertility to the earth by producing rainfall. In some legends, the horned snake was responsible for creating great floods which covered the land.

Legends exist in the southwest of giant snakes that were fed rabbits and cornmeal by some tribes. Early ethnologist observed snake dances taking place where the handling of live snakes occurred. One pictograph at the Abó Painted Rocks Site shows a large snake emerging from a pot and being handled by a ceremonial dancer. Large natural snake-shaped rock formations also exist which were thought to have supernatural powers. The Hopi carved their canes in the shape of a snake, or water serpent, as represented in one Mountainair petroglyph.

A panel which shows a coiled snake associated with a four pointed star that has a face, legs and feet, may represent the Sky or Star God in the Hopi Sun Worship ritual which was performed to bring warmth and rainfall for production of crops, especially corn. Many of the panels in the Mountainair area show stalks of corn bearing ears and tassels. Corn was most important to the Pueblo Indians, not only as a food source but also ceremonially, and was included in almost every aspect of their life. From the number of solar symbols present it appears inhabitants of the area observed and recorded the heavens; one reason may have been for agricultural purposes.

Mother Corn, also found among the Western Pueblos, appears portrayed on one panel associated with a corn plant. The large breasted female symbol appears to be engaged in intercourse (being fertilized) with a male figure directly behind her. Her round head and beak may represent Bird Woman, known as Corn Mother among the Acoma. Mother Corn told the people that the corn would nourish them as milk from her breast. These symbols can indicate reproduction of corn to feed her people thus establishing the continuation of life.

Also associated with corn and its growth is the flute player Kokopelli, or Locust, who was responsible for the Hopi, Acoma, and Sia emergence from the underworld. Locust, playing his flute, is found on flute tiles of the Hopi where he plays over hills of corn and connecting squares which resemble "waffle gardens." These garden plots, found near prehistoric Mountainair ruins, were designed to retain moisture from rainfall since many of the Pueblo Indians had no source of irrigation. The flute player is associated with snake and crane symbols which represent moisture. Flutes from leg bones of the sandhill crane were found in the excavations at Gran Quivira, approximately 40 miles from Abó Pass and at Abó Mission. One panel shows a cornstalk and to its right a sandhill crane whose leg is being "struck" by a snake, or lightning symbol. This may indicate a flute made from the sandhill crane being used to attract lightning and rain for production of the corn. All of the above symbols indicate the people of the area were concerned with rain ceremonies for the production of crops, especially corn. This was also the case at the Western Pueblos.

The turkey and duck, also important to the Hopi and Zuñis, are found on panels in the area. To the Zuñi, the duck represented the messenger of the gods and one of the rulers of the katchinas. Turkeys, raised in captivity by the Indians, had their feathers utilized for ceremonies and the fowl were presented to the Spanish when they entered the area in 1582. The turkey and duck are often associated with katchinas on panels.

The katchina has a very rich and varied tradition among the Pueblo Indians and are found both as pictographs and petroglyphs with a wide variety of facial features and body decoration. The Abó Painted Rocks Site contains figures with headdresses, jewelry, kilts and, in one case, fringed leggings. These leggings and the buffalo horn headdresses are representative of the plains traditions with whom the Southwest people have a history of commerce. However, some cases of facial decoration may represent actual people since Spanish records of 1598 and 1634 recorded tattooing and referred to the people as "Rayados de Jumanos," Juamanos relating to a general term for Indians who used a form of body decoration.

Some of the symbols of masks in the area are associated with canes, or staffs that were widely used among the Western Pueblo Indians. In some Pueblo groups the staff denoted a symbol of authority, thus if a village leader did not posses his cane his orders were ignored as his authority was lacking. Canes were often presented at ceremonies, remained with that person throughout his life and accompanied him at his burial.

A number of katchina symbols appear to represent birds with some holding shields and spears. Most of the shields are the large body type. One petroglyph shows two figures with bison horn headdresses and one with small hand shields, reported to be very rare in the area. A couple of large painted shields are similar to those of the Zuñi Sumaikoli Society, which is associated with the Beast Gods, and may represent protection for the people and villages from warfare, which the residents experienced from Apache raids. Other panels show figures with bows, quivers full of arrows, clubs, and spears. Some of these may be actual hunting representations as one figure is drawing back on his bow and aiming at a lion.

Two other symbols in the area that relate to the Western Pueblo Indians are the Hopi hair whorls on figures and the heart lines on animals which are a distinctive Zuñi trait found painted on their pottery.

One panel of agricultural symbols contains enclosures, or garden spaces, a corn stalk, plants, one Shalako, hand and footprints, a canine figure, a turkey, a coiled snake and recurved bows, among other petroglyphs. The garden spaces located in the Mountainair area were used to retain moisture for crops and their stone outlines may still be seen today. The Shalako is associated with crops and prosperity for the people. Longhorns, also on the panel, bring the warm days and sweeps away the old year. The Longhorns present have one round eye, so the witch people will have a short life, and one long eye so the good people will live a long life. Longhorns also told migration stories, advised when to plant the corn, and acted as war chiefs. Recurved bows on the panel may represent the Bow Chiefs who could also act as a war chief and were in charge of the cornfields.

A number of symbols on the agricultural panel are pecked, denoting "wet." Major dry spells were experienced in the Southwest every two hundred years, forcing people to relocate due to crop failure. One occurred in the 1600s when this area was populated. One cornstalk on the panel appears dead as its roots are showing and no ears of corns are present, plus the field next to it is barren. The "wet" symbols are perhaps associated with ceremonies appealing for rainfall. The pecked coyote, also referred to as water coyote, with his mouth open may be calling the rain, one of his attributes.

In conclusion the above associations provide evidence connecting the Mountainair area with the Hopi and Zuñi Indians and shows they shared a number of common beliefs, ceremonies, and ideas. These cultural similarities may have been absorbed when the pueblo people of the area fled to the Western Pueblos to escape the Spanish domination or through other friendly contact over the years, or both. These beliefs became a part of the residents of the area and offer us important insights into their lives.

Glossary

ABORIGINAL the original native people of an area

A.D. after the death of Christ

ADOBE sun-dried material of earth and straw/organic material

ANASAZI Navajo for "ancient ones" and applies to prehistoric people of the plateau area of the SW which includes the Four Corners region

ANTHROPOLOGY the study of man

ANTHROPOMORPHIC referring human characteristics to non-human beings

ARCHAEOLOGY study of material remains of the culture of people and past human life

ARTIFACT an object modified by man

ASPERSE to sprinkle

AZTEC Indian tribe from the present day Mexico City

AZURITE mineral consisting of blue carbonate (ore) of copper

B.C. before the birth of Christ

BEAST OR PREY GODS animal guardians of the Father of the Medicine Societies

BLUNDERBUSS having a flaring muzzle

BINDER a substance that causes one object to adhere or stick to another

CARBONIZED burned or charred

CARDINAL DIRECTIONS the four main directions of north, south, east and west

CEREMONIAL formal act or series of rituals performed according to strict customs

CHAIN MAIL flexible armor of metal plates or rings worn by the Spanish explores

CHRONOLOGICAL measuring time by divisions that assign events to proper dates

CIRCA around or about

CULT system of beliefs and rituals

CUPULES cup-shaped depressions pecked to various depths in rock

DEITY having supernatural powers

DESERT VARNISH (patina) natural darkening of exposed rock surfaces due to oxides

DEW CLAWS small upper claw on an animal not reaching the ground when it walks

DROUGHT prolonged period of dryness

EPIPHANY the appearance of a divine being

EQUINOX one of the two times a year when the sun crosses the equator making day and night of equal length

ETHNOLOGY the study of the characteristics of a culture

EUROPEAN CONTACT when the Spanish arrived in the southwest (late 1500s–early 1600s)

FETISH an object believed to have magical or protective powers

FAMINE a time of starvation due to scarcity of food or crops

GERMINATION to reproduce or grow

HAWIKUH Native American village built on the eastern side of the Zuni River Valley, it is estimated construction was from A.D. 1300 until A.D. 1680

HAWIKUH POLYCHROME ceramic vessels (pottery) from Hawikuh with three or more colors of paint

HOHOKAM prehistoric people living in the southern part of Arizona

HOPI American Indians living on mesas tops in northeast Arizona, Hopi means "peaceful ones"

JORNADO MOGOLLON prehistoric people who lived in west-central N MEX and east-central AZ

KAOLIN a fine white clay

KATCHINA (may also be spelled katcina) supernatural or ancestral spirits

KIVA Pueblo Indian ceremonial structure that may be either partially or completely underground

KOSHARE (or Qo-sha-re) ceremonial figure

LICHEN alga or fungus growing on a rock surface

LINGUISTICS study of human speech or languages

LITHIC relating to rock or stone tools

LONGHORNS a mask or katchina with one or two long horns attached to its head

MANGANESE hard metallic element that resembles iron

MATASKI POLYCHROME ceramics (pottery) from the Native American village of Hawikuh decorated with three or more colors of paint

MESO AMERICA the land connecting North and South America

MICRON one millionth of a meter

MICROBASIN a very small shallow area

MIMBRES prehistoric people who occupied an area from SW New Mexico from the Mimbres Valley to the Upper Gila drainage to the Mexican border; their realistic paintings of humans, animals and insects on pottery bowls make them highly prized

MONTEZUMA Aztec emperor killed during the Spanish conquest of Mexico

MYTHOLOGY the study of myths or legends which may involve supernatural beings

NEGATIVE PAINTING painting around an object so it is outlined but the object itself is not filled in

OBSIDIAN volcanic glass, usually black

OVERHANG vacant area underneath a rock, boulder or cliff which may be large enough to build in

PAHO a prayerstick

PALEO early or ancient

PATINA another word for desert varnish; a natural darkening of an exposed rocks surface due to naturally occurring oxides

PETROGLYPH pecking, scratching or abrading of a rocks surface

PICTOGRAPH paint applied to a (rock) surface

PIKI paper-thin bread made from blue cornmeal and water

PLUMED SERPENT snake or serpent with a feathered headdress

POLLEN very fine plant seed or spores appearing as a fine dust

POLYCHROME three or more colors

POTTERY vessels made of clay ware and may or may not be fired

POT SHERD fragment of a pottery vessel

POSITIVE PAINTING filling in the outline of a form with paint

PRAYERSTICK a stick to which feathers and other sacred objects may be attached

PREHISTORIC usually refers to before European written history

PUEBLO Spanish word for "town" or "city"; communal dwellings of SW American Indians

PUEBLO INDIAN: There are 19 Pueblo Indian cultures of the Southwest; three of these are the Western Pueblos of Acoma, Laguna and Zuni. The rest are the Eastern Pueblos and are clustered near the Rio Grande River from Toas in the north south to the Mexican border and consist of Cochiti, Isleta, Jemez, Laguna, Nambe, Ohkay, Owingeh, Pojoaque, Sandia, San Felipe, San Ildefonse, Santa Ana, Santa Clara, Santa Domingo, Tesuque and Zia (or Sia).

QUADRUPED having four legs or four feet

REGALIA special dress or finery worn at ceremonies or pow wows

RELATIVE DATES determine the order of events, not the actual date the event occurred

RITUAL established form of a ceremony

ROCK ART term commonly used for petroglyphs and pictographs

ROCK INCORPORATION a natural rock feature giving a petroglyph or pictograph added meaning

ROCK SHELTER an open space under an overhanging rock or boulder

SALADO Prehistoric American Indians that lived in south central and south eastern Arizona

SALINAS Spanish word meaning "salt"

SCAPULA shoulder blade

SERPENTINE winding, turning or zig-zagging one way or another

SHALAKO ceremonial figure 10 to 12 feet tall who carries prayersticks or offerings

SHRINE a spot in which sacred objects may be placed as offerings

SIPAPU a small opening to the underworld in the floor of a kiva

SOCIETY a group with common beliefs and interests

SOLSTICE solar ecliptic point occurring twice a year which marks the beginning of summer and the begining of winter

SOMIKOLI or SHUMIKLOI (spelled either way) Zuni Dragonfly Society

SPALLING flaking off of sections

SUPERNATURAL departing from what is normal or the laws of nature

SUPERIMPOSITION painting over an older or previously painted area or symbol

SYMBOL a sign or object having cultural significance

TABOO forbidden or banned

TOLTEC prehistoric Indians of Casas Grandes, Mexico

TURQUOISE a mineral that may be blue, bluish green or green and forms in copper deposits

VIA by way of

VISION QUEST to seek or conceive an answer or information in a dream or trance

WALPI American Indians living south of the Grand Canyon

YELLOW ORCHRE mixture of the yellow mineral limonite with clay to produce pigment

References Cited

Adams, Charles E.
1991   The Origins and Development of the Pueblo Katsina Cult. The University of Arizona Press, Tucson.

Baldwin, Stuart, J.
1988   A Brief History on the Piro-Tompiro Archaeologyand Ethnohistory Project, 1981 Field Season; Excavations and Archaeological Survey in the Abo Pass Area. The University of Calgary. Calgary Canada. Dept. of Archaeology.

Bancroft, Hubert H.
1889   The Works of Hubert Howe Bancroft Volume XVII History of Arizona and New Mexico, 1530-1888. The History Company, Publishers. McGraw-Hill Book Company, New York.

Bandelier, Adolph F.
1966   (1880-1882) The Southwestern Journals of Adolph F. Bandelier , edited and annotated by C.H.Lange, C.L Riley. The University of New Mexico, Albuquerque.
1975   (1885-1888) The Southwestern Journals of Adolp F. Bandelier, edited and annotated by C.H. Lange, C.L. Riley, and E. M. Lange. University of New Mexico Press, Albuquerque.

Bol, Marsha C.
1998   Stars Above Earth Below. Roberts Rinehart Publishers, Niwot, Colorado.

Bourke, John G.
1884   The Snake Dance of the Moquis of Arizona. Charles Scribner's Sons, New York.

Brandt, John C. and Ray A. Williamson
1977   Rock Art Representations of the A. D. 1054 Supernova: A Progress Report. In Native American Astronomy. University of Texas Press, Austin and London.

Branson, Ocsar T.
1992   Hopi Indian Kachina Dolls. Treasure Chest Publications, Inc., Tucson, Arizona.

Brody, J. J.
1991   Anasazi and Pueblo Painting. University of New Mexico Press, Albuquerque.

Bunzel, Ruth L.
1973   (1929-1939)Zuši Katcinas. Forty-Seventh Annual Report of the Bureau of American Ethnology, Washington, D.C. Reprinted by The Rio Grande Press, Inc., Glorieta, New Mexico.
1992   Zuni Ceremonialism. University of New Mexico Press, Albuquerque.

Chamberlain, Von Del
1982   When Stars Came Down to Earth, Cosmology of the Skidi Pawnee Indians of North America. Ballena Press Anthropological Papers No. 26. Los Altos, CA.

Chartrand III, Mark R.
1982   Skyguide. Golden Press, New York.

Cole, Sally J.
1984   The Abo Painted Rocks Documentation and Analysis. A report prepared for Salinas National Monument New Mexico. Research was funded by Southwest Parks and Monuments Association.

Colton, Harold S.
1959   Hopi Kachina Dolls. University of New Mexico Press, Albuquerque. (originally published 1949)

Courlander, Harold (recorder, transcriber, annotator)
1982   Hopi Voices. University of New Mexico Press, Albuquerque.

Curtis, Edward S.
1970   The North American Indian VOL. XII-a. Johnson
        Reprint Corporation, New York. N.Y.
1970   The North American Indian VOL. XVI. Johnson
        Reprint Corporation, New York, N.Y.

Cushing, Frank H.
1994   (1883) Zuni Fetiches. Second Annual Report of the
        Bureau of Ethnology. Government Printing Office.
        Washington.
1979   Zuni. University of Nebraska Press. Lincoln and
        London.
1988   The Mythic World of the Zuni. University of New
        Mexico Press. Alburquerque.

Dorsey, George A.
1904   The Mythology of the Wichita. Carnegie Institution
        of Washington, Publication No. 21. Washington D.C.
        Reprinted by the University Of Oklahoma Press,
        Norman.
1971   The Cheyenne. Field Columbian Museum,
        Anthropological Series. Publication 99, Vol. IX, No.1.
        The Rio Grande Press, Inc. Glorieta, New Mexico.

Dutton, Bertha P.
1963   Sun Father's Way, The Kiva Murals of Kuaua. The
        University of New Mexico Press, Albuquerque.

Elmore, Francis H.
1976   Shrubs and Trees of the Southwest Uplands. Southwest
        Parks and Monuments Association. Popular Series
        No.19. Tucson, Arizona.

Ferguson T.J. and E. Richard Hart
1985   A Zuni Atlas. University of Norman Press: Norman and
        London.

Fewkes, J. Walter
1900   Hopi Snake Ceremonies: Tusayan Snake Ceremonies.
        Sixteenth Annual Report of the Bureau of American
        Ethnology. Government Printing Office, Washington,
        pages 267-312. Tusayan Flute Snake Ceremonies,
        Part 2. Nineteeth Annual Report of the Bureau
        of American Ethnology. Government Printing,
        Washington, pages 959- Reprinted.
1903   (1899-1900) Hopi Katchinas. Twenty-First Annual
        Report of the Bureau of American Ethnology.
        Washington. Government Printing Office.

1920   (1918) Sun Worship of the Hopi Indians. Annual Report
       of the Board of Regents of the Smithsonian Institution.
       Washington Government Printing Office.

1973   Designs on Prehistoric Hopi Pottery. Dover
       Publications, Inc., New York.

1900   Tusayan Katcinas and Hopi Altars. Avanya Publishing,
       Inc., Albuquerque, New Mexico.

Fleisher Martin, T. Liu, W. S. Broecker, and W. Moore

1999   A clue regarding the origin of rock varnish. Geophysical
       Reserach Letters, Vol. 26, No.1: 103-106. 2000 Florida
       Ave., NW. Washington, DC.

Griffin-Pierce, Trudy

1992   The Hooghan and the Stars. In Earth & Sky, edited by
       R.A. Williamson C. R. Farrer, pp. 110-129. University
       of New Mexico Press, Albuquerque.

Hawley, Marlin F.

2000   European-contact and Southwestern Artifacts in the
       Lower Walnut Focus Sites at Arkansas City, Kansas.
       Plains Anthropologist, Vol.45, No.173, pp.237-255.

Hays, Alden C., J.H. Young, and A.H. Warren

1981   Excavation of Mound 7, Grand Quiveria National
       Monument, New Mexico. U.S. Printing Office,
       Washington, D.C.

Hays, Kelly Ann

1994   Kachina Depictions on Prehistoric Pueblo Pottery.
       In Kachinas in the Pueblo World, edited by Polly
       Schaafsma, pp.47-62. University of New Mexico Press,
       Albuquerque.

Hibben, Frank C.

1975   Kiva Art of the Anasazi at Pottery Mound. K C
       Publications, Las Vegas, Nevada.

Hodge, Frederick W.

1912   Handbook of American Indians North of Mexico.
       Part 1. Washington Government Printing Office.

Hodge, F. W.,G.P.Hammond, and A. Rey

1945   Fray Alonso de Benavidas' Revised Memorial of 1634.
       University of New Mexico Press, Albuquerque.

Holland, Susan A.

1998   Evidence of the Spring Planting Ceremony to Evening
       Star and Her Sacred Garden. Plains Anthropologist, Vol.
       43, No. 166, pp 411-418.

Hrdlicka, Ales
1908   Physiological and Medical Observations. Bureau of American Ethnology, Bulletin 34. Government Printing Office, Washington.

Lange, Charles H.
1959   Cochiti A New Mexico Pueblo, Past and Present. University of New Mexico Press. Albuquerque.

LeBlanc, Steven A.
1999   Prehistoric Warfare in the American Southwest. The University of Utah Press, Salt Lake City.

Liu, Tanzhuo, W.S.Broecher.
2000   How fast does rock varnish grow? Geology Vol. 28, No. 2:183-186. Geological Society of America, Inc. Boulder, Colorado.

Lowie, Robert H.
1982   Indians of the Plains. University of Nebraska Press.

Luckert, Karl W.
1979   Coyoteway a Navajo Holyway Healing Ceremonial. University of Arizona Press, Tucson and the Museum of Northern Arizona Press, Flagstaff.

Mallery, Garrick
1972   (1893)Picture-Writing of the American Indian, Volume Two. Tenth Annual Report of the Bureau of Ethnology, Washington, D.C. Reprinted by Dover Publications Inc., New York.

Martineau, LaVan
1973   The Rocks Begin To Speak. KC Publications, Las Vegas.
1992   Southern Paiutes, Legends Lore Language and Lineage. KC Publications, Las Vegas.
1996   The Legacy of the Giants. Martineau Video Productions. Globe, Arizona.

Miles, Charles
1973   Indian and Eskimo Artifacts of North America. Bonanza Books, New York.

Miller, Dorcas S.
1997   Stars of the First People. Pruett Publishing Company, Boulder, Colorado.

Miller, Millie and C. Nelson
1987   Hummers, hummingbirds of north america. Johnson Books, Boulder.

Murie, James R.
 1981   Ceremonies of the Pawnee, Part I: The Skiri.
          Smithsonian Institution Press, Washington D.C.
          Reprinted by the University of Nebraska Press, Lincoln.

Murphy, Dan
 1982   Salinas Archaeology History Prehistory. McLeod
          Printing Company, Albuquerque, New Mexico.
 1993   Salinas Pueblo Missions. Southwest Parks and
          Monuments Association, Tucson, Arizona.

Nequatewa, Edmund
 1954   HOPI HOPIWIME: The Hopi Ceremonial Calendar.
          HOPI CUSTOMS, FOLKLORE, AND CEREMONIES.
          Reprint Series No. 4, Museum of Northern Arizona,
          Flagstaff.

Nicholson, Irene
 1985   (1967) Mexican and Central American Mythology.
          Peter Bedrick Books. New York.

Parsons, Elsie C.
 1966   (1936)Pueblo Indian Religion, Volume 1. University of
          Nebraska Press, Lincoln.
 1966   (1936)Pueblo Indian Religion, Volume 2. University of
          Nebraska Press, Lincoln.

Rice, Glen E.
 1993   Eagles and Lions: Toward A Salado Iconography.
          Hohokam News February Volume 7, Number 1.

Schaafsma, Curtis F.
 1994   Pueblo Ceremonialism from the Perspective of Spanish
          Documents. In Kachinas in the Pueblo World, edited
          by Polly Schaafsma, pp. 121-137. University of New
          Mexico Press, Albuquerque.

Schaafsma, Polly
 1994   The Prehistoric Kachina Cult and Its Origins as
          Suggested by Southwestern Rock Art. In Kachinas in
          the Pueblo World, edited by Polly Schaafsma, pp.63-79.
          University of New Mexico Press, Albuquerque.
 2000   Warrior, Shield, and Star. Western Ridge Press.

Scriver, Bob
 1990   The Blackfoot Artists of the Northern Plains. The
          Lowell Press, Inc. Kansas City, MO.

Slifer, Dennis and J. Duffield
 1994   Kokopelli Flute Player Images in Rock Art. Ancient
          Cities Press, Santa Fe, New Mexico.

Smith Watson, Richard B. Woodbury, and Nathalie F.S. Woodbury

1966   The Excavation of Hawikuh by Frederick Webb Hodge. Museum of the American Indian, Heye Foundation, New York.

Stephen Alexander M.

1936   Hopi Journal Part I. Edited by E C Parsons. Columbia University Press, New York.

Stevenson, Matilda C.

1894   The Sia. Bureau of Ethnology, 11th Annual Report, Washington.

1904   The Zuni Indians-Their Mythology, Esoteric Fraternities and Ceremonies. Bureau of American Ethnology, 23rd Annual Report, Washington.

1915   (1908-1909) Ethnobotany of the Zuni Indians. Bureau of American Ethnology, 30th Annual Report, Washington.

Sturtevant, William C,

1979   Handbook of North American Indians. Smithsonian Institution, Washington.

Swanton, John R.

1984   The Indian Tribes of North America. Smithsonian Institution Bureau of American Ethnology, Bulletin 145. City of Washington. Originally printed 1952.

Sweet, Jill D.

1985   Dances of the Tiwa Pueblo Indians. School of American Research Press, Santa Fe, New Mexico.

Tanner, Clara Lee

1976   Prehistoric Southwestern Craft Arts. The University of Arizona Press, Tucson, Arizona.

Taube, Karl

1993   Aztec and Maya Myths. British Museum Press, University of Texas Press, Austin.

Titiev, Mischa

1992   Old Oraibi A Study of the Hopi Indians of Third Mesa. University of New Mexico Press, Albuquerque.

Tyler, Hamilton A.

1964   Pueblo Gods and Myths. University of Oklahoma Press, Norman.

U. Bar Verlag
1989 Pueblos. Copyrighted, Switzerland. Original title: Die Pueblos-Translated Copy 1990 by Facts on Life, Inc. Maximilien Bruggman, Sylvio Acatos.

Vivian, Gordon
1979 Gran Quivera. Archeological Research Series Number Eight, National Park Service, U.S. Department of the Interior.

Vogel, Virgil J.
1970 American Indian Medicine. University of Oklahoma Press, Norman and London.

Voth, H. R.
1905 The Traditions of the Hopi. Field Columbian Museum, Publication 96, Anthropological Series, Vol. VIII, Chicago, U.S.A.

Wade, Edwin L.
1986 The Arts of the North American Indian. Edited by Edwin L. Wade. Hudson Hills Press, New York.

Waters, Frank
1950 Masked Gods Navajo and Pueblo Ceremonialism. The Swallow Press Inc., Chicago.

Wedel, Mildred M.
1988 The Wichita Indians 1541-1750 Ethnohistorical Essays. Reprints in Anthropology, Volume 38. J & L Reprint Company, Lincoln, Nebraska.

Wormington, H. M.
1957 Ancient Man in North America. The Denver Museum of Natural History, Denver, Colorado.

Wright, Barton
1976 Pueblo Shields. Northland Press, Flagstaff, Arizona.
1977 Hopi Kachinas. Northland Press, Flagstaff, Arizona.
1979 Hopi Material Culture. Northland Press, Flagstaff, Arizona.
1994 The Changing Kachina. In Kachinas in the Pueblo World, edited by Polly Schaafsma, pp. 139-146. University of New Mexico Press, Albuquerque.

Young, M.J.
1988 Signs From The Ancestors. University of New Mexico Press, Albuquerque.
1994 The Interconnection Between Western Puebloan and Mesoamerican Ideology/Cosmology. In Kachinas in the Pueblo World, edited by Polly Schaafsma, pp. 107-120. University of New Mexico Press, Albuquerque.

Twin Snakes
Messengers of the Rain Gods

Flute Player
Brings Rain for crops

Duck
Messenger and God

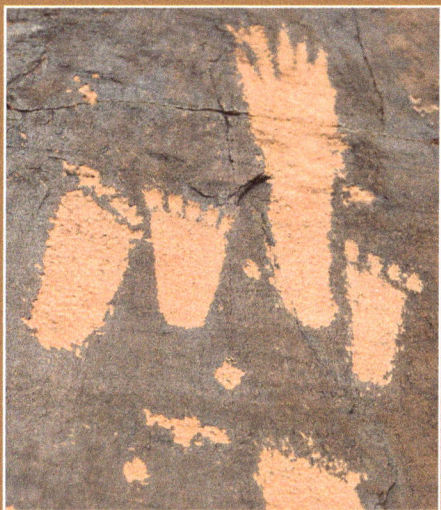

Footprints
People on a long journey

Eagle - Zuni Warrior God
Associated with a Pure Heart

Deer Leg with Dew Claw
Indicates danger or fleeing

Head with Feathers
Power to see and hear

Footprints
Danger or exposed

Petroglyphs of Central New Mexico

Zuni Serpent and Sky God
Serpent brings rain, Sun brings warmth

Pronghorn
Climbing uphill

Mountain Lion—Zuni Prey God
"Heart Line" is for a successful hunt

Face or Mask
Eagle Clan

Shamen—Strong Medicine, Powerful
Small hand shield—very rare

Petroglyphs of Central New Mexico